THIRTY H
OF TI
WESLEYS

David and Jill Wright

EXETER
THE PATERNOSTER PRESS

AUSTRALIA:
Bookhouse Australia Ltd.,
P.O. Box 115, Flemington Markets, NSW 2129

SOUTH AFRICA:
Oxford University Press,
P.O. Box 1141, Cape Town

British Library Cataloguing in Publication Data

Wright, David
Thirty Hymns of the Wesleys
1. Hymns, English
I. Title II. Wright, Jill
264'.2 BV459

ISBN 0-85364-414-4

Typeset by Photoprint, 9-11 Alexandra Lane, Torquay and Printed and Bound in Great Britain for The Paternoster Press, Paternoster House, 3 Mount Radford Crescent, Exeter, Devon by A. Wheaton & Co. Ltd, Exeter

Contents

By the same authors:
Praise with Understanding: an encounter with Thirty Hymns

To W. S. Wright

PREFACE

My heart is full of Christ, and longs
Its glorious matter to declare!
Of him I make my loftier songs,
I cannot from his praise forbear;
My ready tongue makes haste to sing
The glories of my heavenly King.

This opening verse of Charles Wesley's paraphrase of Psalm 45 admirably sums up his life and work. The Wesleys—Samuel (Senior) and his three sons, Samuel, John and Charles—all wrote hymns; Charles alone wrote over 6,000 hymns. Hence, for every one hymn in this book, there are over 200 not included.

This book is neither another study of the Wesleys, nor a general survey of Wesleyan hymnody, nor an analysis of the literary merit of the hymns. Its scope is deliberately much more limited. We have made a varied selection of 30 hymns, and for these hymns we have sought both the inner message and the probable sources of inspiration. The main source is the Bible—in the King James Version familiar to the Wesleys; but they also referred to the Book of Common Prayer, the writings of the Early Fathers, contemporary poets and other literary sources. We have deliberately included some forgotten or little-known hymns, as well as some of the most popular ones. Hundreds of other hymns cried out for inclusion: we hope that this small volume will encourage further study.

The comments on the first six are linked with some of the major events in the lives of the Wesleys. Hymns 7 to 12 are hymns on the Christian Year, while the remaining hymns cover a wide variety of Christian themes. There are hymns by Samuel (Sr.) (p.6); Samuel (Jr.) (p.8), and translations from the German by John Wesley (pp.12, 34 and 48). The remaining 25 are probably by Charles Wesley, although some scholars attribute a few of them to John.

In several cases, we have included more verses than are usually sung today. However, we have not pedantically sought to reproduce the exact words of the original in every case. Where a revised form is widely used, we have used the revision, for hymns are a living form of worship, not a dead form of words.

A major reason for undertaking this work is our concern that hymns which were originally written to clarify the faith have themselves become almost incomprehensible. We have found the work full of interest and most rewarding, and we would recommend the study of hymns as a valuable—and sadly neglected—form of Christian activity.

David and Jill Wright,
Mulbarton, Norfolk.

Scripture references are shown in italics. Verse and line references to hymns appear thus: (v.2.1).

O THOU WHO WHEN I DID COMPLAIN, DIDST ALL MY GRIEF REMOVE

"I was brought low, and he helped me"
(*Psalm 116:6*)

---

1 O Thou who, when I did complain,
Didst all my griefs remove,
O Saviour, do not now disdain
My humble praise and love.

2 Since thou a pitying ear didst give,
And hear me when I prayed,
I'll call upon thee while I live,
And never doubt thy aid.

3 Pale death, with all his ghastly train,
My soul encompassed round,
Anguish, and sin, and dread, and pain,
On every side I found.

4 To thee, O Lord of life, I prayed,
And did for succour flee:
O save (in my distress I said)
The soul that trusts in thee!

5 How good thou art! how large thy grace!
How ready to forgive!
The helpless thou delight'st to raise:
And by thy love I live.

6 Then, O my soul, be never more
With anxious thoughts distrest!
God's bounteous love doth thee restore
To ease, and joy, and rest.

7 My eyes no longer drowned in tears,
My feet from falling free,
Redeemed from death and guilty fears,
O Lord, I'll live to thee.

The author of this hymn is Samuel Wesley (1662-1735), father of Samuel (Jr.), John and Charles Wesley—and also of 16 other children, of whom only seven daughters survived infancy.

Samuel Wesley was a remarkable man. His father, John Westley, was imprisoned in 1661 for refusing to use the Prayer Book, and was ejected from the Church of England in 1662. He became a Nonconformist pastor at Poole, and Samuel was educated at Dissenting academies. But he decided to rejoin the Church of England, and was thus able to complete his education at Oxford. In 1689 he was ordained and he married Susannah Annesley. Her father had also been ejected from the Church of England to become a Nonconformist pastor, but at the age of 13 Susannah determined to join the established church.

From 1697 until his death, Samuel Wesley was Rector of Epworth in Lincolnshire. Samuel was a conscientious parson—quite exceptionally so at a time when many parsons were notoriously slack at undertaking even the minimum of their duties. He preached long sermons; he encouraged his parishioners to attend Communion frequently; and he criticized loose living and loose thinking. His son, John, wrote of him: "My father's method was to visit all his parishioners, sick or well, from house to house, to talk with each of them on the things of God and observe severally the state of their souls. What he observed he minuted down in a book kept for that purpose . . .". Such conscientiousness made him unpopular in the parish, and a number of people thought that the fires which twice threatened the Rectory—the 1709 one nearly engulfing the family—were started deliberately.

The hymn is a much freer rendering of Psalm 116 than was normal at the time when it was written, and includes some fine lines. The least satisfying line is the first—which may account for the absence of this hymn from most current hymnbooks.

This hymn was originally published, with some other versions of Psalms, in Samuel Wesley's "Pious Communicant Rightly Prepared" (1700). John Wesley included this and several other hymns by his father in his first hymnbook, "Collection of Psalms and Hymns", which he published in Charlestown in 1737—the first hymnbook to be published in America.

The first five verses take the themes of the corresponding verses in the Psalm, and expand them in the light of the New Testament. Thus v.1 of the Psalm, "I love the Lord", becomes a prayer to the 'Saviour' (v.1.3). The author thanks the Saviour for past blessings (v.1.1-2): "he hath heard my voice and my supplications" (*Ps. 116:1*), and asks for his praise and love to be acceptable (v.1.3-4).

The confident, joyful statement in *Psalm 116:2* (v.2.3) "I will call upon Him as long as I live", is in contrast with the tragic picture in verses 3 and 4 of both Psalm and hymn. Samuel Wesley has accurately captured the sudden change of mood that characterizes this Psalm. "The sorrows of death compassed me, and the pains of hell gat hold upon me: I found trouble and sorrow" (*Ps. 116:3;* v.3 of hymn). "Then called I upon the name of the Lord; O Lord, I beseech thee, deliver my soul" (*Ps. 116:4;* v.4 of hymn). The answered prayer has already been mentioned in the first two verses of the hymn—but the dramatic change that the answered prayer made to the Psalmist's life is well expressed in v.5: "Gracious is the Lord, and righteous; yea, our God is merciful . . . I was brought low, and he helped me" (*Psalm 116:5-6;* v.5 of hymn). The last line of verse 5 of the hymn, 'And by thy love I live' is particularly memorable. It is partly based on v.9 of the Psalm, "I will walk before the Lord in the land of the living". God's love is implicit in the Psalm, but is twice made explicit in the hymn (v.5.4 and v.6.3).

The theme of praise continues: "the Lord hath dealt bountifully with thee" (*Ps. 116:7;* hymn v.6); "Thou hast delivered my soul from death, mine eyes from tears, and my feet from falling" (*Ps. 116:8;* hymn v.7). Thus the hymn ends on a triumphant note. We praise our Saviour for redeeming us from death and fears (v.7.3), and conclude "O Lord, I'll live to thee" (v.7.4). These themes can partly be traced to the last three verses of *Psalm 116*, but the expressions are of a full New Testament faith.

HAIL FATHER, WHOSE CREATING CALL UNNUMBERED WORLDS ATTEND

"In the beginning, God . . ."

(*Genesis 1:1*)

1 Hail, Father, whose creating call
Unnumbered worlds attend;
Jehovah, comprehending all,
Whom none can comprehend!

2 In light unsearchable enthroned,
Whom angels dimly see,
The fountain of the Godhead owned,
And foremost of the Three.

3 From thee, through an eternal now,
The Son, thine offspring, flowed;
An everlasting Father thou,
An everlasting God.

4 Nor quite displayed to worlds above,
Nor quite on earth concealed;
By wondrous, unexhausted love,
To mortal man revealed.

5 Supreme and all-sufficient God,
When nature shall expire.
And worlds created by thy nod
Shall perish by thy fire.

6 Thy name, Jehovah, be adored
By creatures without end,
Whom none but thy essential Word
And Spirit comprehend.

Samuel Wesley, Junior (1691-1739), was the oldest child of Samuel and Susannah Wesley. He was 12 years old when John was born, and by then he was away from home at Westminster School, where he was educated before going to Oxford University. He was ordained, and returned to Westminster School as a teacher, while his youngest brother, Charles, was still a pupil at the school. By this time John was at Charterhouse, and he lodged with Samuel during the school holidays. From 1732 until his death in 1739, Samuel was headmaster of Tiverton Free School, Devonshire. The epitaph in Tiverton churchyard describes him as "A man, for his uncommon wit and learning, for the benevolence of his temper, and simplicity of manners, deservedly loved and esteemed by all: An excellent preacher; but whose best sermon was the constant example of an edifying life . . .".

Samuel Wesley Jr. wrote several hymns, but few are known today. This hymn is one of a trilogy. It is entitled "Hymn to God the Father". His "Hymn to God the Son" begins "Hail God the Son, in glory crowned", and his "Hymn to the Holy Spirit" begins "Hail, Holy Ghost". Each had six verses and used the Common Metre.

This hymn was originally published on the first page of his "Collection of Poems on Several Occasions", 1736. Although Samuel did not sympathize with his brothers' evangelistic work, John and Charles admired much of their elder brother's poetry, and John included this and other hymns by Samuel in his "Collection of Psalms and Hymns" published in Charlestown, America, in 1737. It was not included in his 1780 hymnbook, though added in the 1831 supplement. It was also printed in a number of Anglican hymnbooks, including 'Hymns Ancient and Modern' (Standard Edition), sometimes with minor amendments by editors.

The distinctive message and relatively simple language of this hymn make it worthy of rediscovery, for there are few hymns "To God the Father" in most hymnbooks today. The hymn speaks first of God as Creator. We now know that the 'unnumbered worlds' (v.1.2) are far more numerous than the Wesleys could have imagined. In this verse, and in the last, Samuel Wesley speaks of God as Jehovah (v.1.3; v.6.1). God revealed this name for himself to Moses (*Exodus 6:2-3*). God the Creator, the self-existing Jehovah, comprehends all (v.1.3) but is himself incomprehensible (v.1.4). There is a subtle play on the word 'comprehend' here—God both understands all things and encompasses all things. This is a reference, too, to the Athanasian Creed: "The Father incomprehensible . . .". Not only is God beyond our understanding, but beyond our sight (v.2.1): ". . . dwelling in the light which no man can approach unto; whom no man hath seen nor can see . . ." (*1 Timothy 6:16*). God is hidden even from the angels of heaven—when Isaiah saw a vision of God enthroned in glory, he also saw seraphim who covered their faces from the sight of God (v.2.2; *Isaiah 6:1-2*). At the end of this verse we return again to doctrines expressed in the creed of St. Athanasius: "The Father is made of none . . . The Son is of the Father . . . begotten. The Holy Ghost is of the Father and of the Son . . . proceeding". The last line has been altered in some versions to "First-named among the three"; a rendering that is more in tune with the affirmation from the same creed "And in this Trinity none is afore, or after other: none is greater, or less than another".

Verse 3 continues to express the relationship of God the Father and God the Son. Few hymns successfully explore the meaning of God beyond time: the phrase 'an eternal now' (v.3.1) is striking and helpful.

Verse 4 moves on to God's revelation of himself, without which he would be unknown to man. "He left not himself without witness, in that he did good, and gave us rain from heaven, and fruitful seasons, filling our hearts with food and gladness" (v.4.2; *Acts 14:17*; see also *Romans 1:20*). 'Wondrous, unexhausted love' (v.4.3) is the source of all God's revelation and the very nature of God himself—supremely seen in Jesus.

Verse 5 concentrates on the 'all-sufficient God' who is not dependent on creation or revelation. When creation is extinguished, when "the elements shall melt with fervent heat, the earth also and the works that are therein shall be burned up" (v.5.3-4; *2 Peter 3:10*), then God remains supreme. The concluding prayer of adoration (v.6) can be interpreted as both the endless praise at the end of the world (the vision of *Revelation 5:7; 21-22*) and the endless praise due to God now from his creation. We praise God, Jehovah, the self-existing creator (v.6.1-2); Jesus, "the Word made flesh" (v.6.3; *John 1:14*); and the Holy Spirit (v.6.4). Only the Son and the Spirit can comprehend God, but we can all worship him.

LONG HAVE I SEEMED TO SERVE THEE, LORD

". . . by the works of the law shall no flesh be justified."
(*Galatians 2:16*)

---

1 Long have I seemed to serve thee, Lord,
With unavailing pain,
Fasted, and prayed, and read thy word,
And heard it preached in vain.

2 Oft did I with the assembly join,
And near thine altar drew;
A form of godliness was mine,
The power I never knew.

3 I rested in the outward law,
Nor knew its deep design;
The length and breadth I never saw,
And height, of love divine.

4 To please thee thus, at length I see,
Vainly I hoped and strove;
For what are outward things to thee,
Unless they spring from love?

5 I see the perfect law requires
Truth in the inward parts,
Our full consent, our whole desires,
Our undivided hearts.

6 But I of means have made my boast,
Of means an idol made;
The spirit in the letter lost,
The substance in the shade.

7 Where am I now, or what my hope?
What can my weakness do?
Jesus, to thee my soul looks up,
'Tis thou must make it new.

This hymn was first published in "Hymns and Sacred Poems" (1740) with 23 verses. John Wesley selected 15 of these for two hymns in his 1780 book. The original long hymn was written at a time when the Wesleys were troubled by Quietists, who taught that all means of grace (including prayer and Bible reading) should be avoided in case Christians came to rely on them for salvation—all that was necessary was to "quietly" wait on God. Wesley drew on his own experience to show the dangers of seeking salvation through "doing", but in later verses showed how true faith would move the Christian to want to use all the means of grace available.

Although the truths of this hymn are firmly rooted in Scripture, it largely describes the personal experience of Charles Wesley and his brother John. There is stress on long service (v.1.1 and v.2.1). The brothers were born into a large and religious family. Their father's faithful ministry has already been described (page 6). Their mother, Susannah, was a very pious woman who made time to teach each of her ten surviving children.

It was while an undergraduate at Oxford that Charles founded the so-called Holy Club. John became the leader when he returned as a lecturer in Classics after serving as his father's curate. Verses 1 and 2 describe the activities of the "Holy Club" well—they met regularly to study the Greek New Testament and various religious books; they fasted on Wednesdays and Fridays; they attended Communion weekly; and they undertook "good works" in the City of Oxford—visiting prisoners and poor families. They were jeered at by others at the University, and among the nicknames given to them, they were called "Methodists". When the Wesleys and some other "Holy Club" members went to America they continued these strict religious observances and encouraged others to do the same, which contributed to their unpopularity there (see next page).

Characteristically, Charles describes their own experience in biblical terms. In v.2, he regrets "having a form of godliness, but denying the power thereof" (*2 Timothy 3:5*). In verse 3, the 'deep design' of the 'outward law' (v.3.1-2) probably refer on the one hand to *Romans 7:5*: ". . . the motion of sins, which were by the law, did work in our members to bring forth fruit unto death"; and on the other hand to *Galatians 3:24*: ". . . the law was our schoolmaster to bring us to Christ . . .". He longs for Paul's prayer to be answered in his own life (v.3.3-4): "that ye . . . may be able to comprehend with all saints what is the breadth, and length, and depth, and height; and to know the love of Christ . . ." (*Ephesians 3:18*). The Bible, which they so diligently read in their attempt to please God, made God's requirements plain (v.5): "Behold, thou desirest truth in the inward parts" (*Psalm 51:6*) and "Thou shalt love the Lord thy God with all thy heart, and with all thy soul, and with all thy mind. This is the first and great commandment" (*Deuteronomy 6:5*; quoted by Jesus in *Matthew 22:37-8*).

Returning to *Romans* 7, Charles Wesley makes use of the next verse to the one quoted above (v.6.3): "But now we are delivered from the law . . . that we should serve in newness of spirit, and not in the oldness of the letter" (*Romans 7:6*). 'The shade' (v.6.4) refers to the Law again: "For the law having a shadow of good things to come, and not the very image of the things, can never with those sacrifices they offered year by year continually make the comers thereunto perfect" (*Hebrews 10:1*). In v.6, he looks back to the time before he knew "newness of spirit"; in v.7 he prays to know this newness (v.4). On page 14 we find him praising God because this prayer has been answered.

THOU HIDDEN LOVE OF GOD . . .

"That ye . . . may be able to comprehend with all saints what is the breadth, and length, and depth, and height. And to know the love of Christ . . ." (*Ephesians 3:18-19*)

---

1 Thou hidden Love of God. Whose height,
Whose depth unfathomed, no man knows,
I see from far Thy beauteous light,
Inly I sigh for Thy repose;
My heart is pained, nor can it be
At rest, till it finds rest in Thee.

2 Thy secret voice invites me still
The sweetness of thy yoke to prove;
And fain I would; but though my will
Seems fixed, yet wide my passions rove;
Yet hindrances strew all the way;
I aim at thee, yet from thee stray.

3 'Tis mercy all that thou has brought
My mind to seek her peace in thee;
Yet, while I seek but find thee not,
No peace my wandering soul shall see;
O when shall all my wanderings end,
And all my steps to thee-ward tend!

4 Is there a thing beneath the sun
That strives with thee my heart to share?
Ah, tear it thence, and reign alone,
The Lord of every motion there!
Then shall my heart from earth be free,
When it hath found repose in thee.

5 O hide this self from me, that I
No more, but Christ in me, may live!
My vile affections crucify,
Nor let one darling lust survive!
In all things nothing may I see,
Nothing desire or seek, but thee!

6 O Love, thy sovereign aid impart,
To save me from low-thoughted care;
Chase this self-will through all my heart,
Through all its latent mazes there,
Make me thy duteous child, that I
Ceaseless may, "Abba, Father," cry!

7 Ah no! ne'er will I backward turn,
Thine wholly, thine alone, I am:
Thrice happy be he who views with scorn
Earth's toys, for thee his constant flame!
O help, that I may never move
From the blest footsteps of thy love!

8 Each moment, draw from earth away
My heart that lowly waits Thy call;
Speak to my inmost soul and say,
"I am thy Love, thy God, thy All!"
To feel Thy power, to hear Thy voice.
To taste Thy love, be all my choice.

This is a translation by John Wesley of the ten-verse hymn *"Verborgne Gottes Liebe du"* by Gerhard Tersteegen. Wesley translated this German hymn in 1736 while living in Savannah, Georgia. He published it in 1738 in "A Collection of Psalms and Hymns". Slightly different versions were published in his later hymn books.

The original German hymn was first published in 1729 in Tersteegen's *'Geistliches Blumengärtlein"*, with the heading "The longing of the soul quietly to maintain the secret drawings of the love of God". John Wesley found it in the hymnal of the Moravians at Herrnhut—the hymnbook of the Moravian community in Georgia. Although his translation can be found in many English hymnbooks, the original hymn was used in Germany only by the early Moravians.

Gerhard Tersteegen (1697-1769) was born at Mörs, in Westphalia. He wrote many hymns, two of which John Wesley translated into English, and others have come to us from later translators.

Shortly after their father's death in 1735, John and Charles Wesley sailed for Georgia, America. Among the other passengers were Protestants from the Christian Community at Herrnhut, Germany, which had been founded by Count Zinzendorf, for Moravian refugees (see page 48). John Wesley started to learn German and was impressed by their faith and life-style. During a great storm in January 1736, the Moravians sang hymns joyfully and calmly, and told him that they were not afraid to die.

Neither of the Wesleys had a happy time in Georgia. Charles' health failed and he suffered bitter personal attacks. He returned home in 1736. John was in Savannah, where he tried to organize the church into an Oxford-style "Holy Club". His efforts were resented, but he stayed until early 1738. Back in London, both brothers kept in touch with Moravians and it was Peter Böhler, a German on his way to missionary work in America, who helped to lead both John and Charles to a personal faith and peace with God (see page 14).

Although a translation, this hymn clearly expresses John Wesley's feelings while he was in Savannah. V.1 opens with an echo of Paul's great prayer for the Ephesian church (*Ephesians 3:14-21*), and quickly moves to personal longing. The last two lines are Wesley's own: one of many instances where he deviates from the original, giving the sense of the author without providing a direct translation. Here, he is deliberately using a famous passage from the Confessions of St. Augustine: "Thou hast made us for Thyself, and our heart is restless, until it finds rest in Thee." This longing continues in the second verse, which opens with a reference to Jesus' invitation, "Come unto me, all ye that labour and are heavy laden and I will give you rest. Take my yoke upon you, and learn of me . . . for my yoke is easy, and my burden is light" (*Matthew 11:28-30*). Like Paul, the author cannot understand his inability to respond (v.2.3-6): "For that which I do I allow not: for what I would, that do I not . . ." (*Romans 7:15*). A similar conflict is expressed in verse 3, where the "wandering soul" (v.3.4-5) knows no peace, and yet "the peace of God, which passeth all understanding, shall keep your hearts and minds through Christ Jesus" (*Philippians 4:7*).

The next three verses are a prayer for God to remove everything that rivals his presence (v.4): all selfishness (v.5) and self-will (v.6). They contain several references to Paul's letter to the Galatians. V.5 combines "I am crucified with Christ. Nevertheless I live, yet not I, but Christ liveth in me" (*Galatians 2:20*) with "And they that are Christ's have crucified the flesh with the affections and lusts" (*Galatians 5:24*). The end of v.6 refers to *Galatians 4:6,* "Because ye are sons, God hath sent forth the spirit of his Son into your hearts, crying Abba, Father."

The final verses speak of salvation received. He has put his hand to the plough and there will be no 'backward turn' (v.7.1 and *Luke 9:62*). Another of Christ's commands will be readily obeyed (v.7.3-4): "Lay not up for yourselves treasures on earth . . ." (*Matthew 6:19*). The prayer of the last verse for ever-increasing communion with God must have been John Wesley's as he sought holiness in Savannah, and continued seeking in London while still in contact with the Moravian Brethren.

AND CAN IT BE THAT I SHOULD GAIN . . .

"... the life which I now live in the flesh I live by the faith of the Son of God, who loved me, and gave himself for me"
(*Galatians 2:20*)

1 And can it be, that I should gain
An interest in the Saviour's blood?
Died he for me, who caused his pain?
For me, who him to death pursued?
Amazing love! how can it be
That thou, my God, shouldst die for me?

2 'Tis mystery all! The Immortal dies!
Who can explore his strange design?
In vain the first-born seraph tries
To sound the depths of love divine!
'Tis mercy all! let earth adore,
Let angel-minds inquire no more.

3 He left his Father's throne above,
(So free, so infinite his grace!)
Emptied himself of all but love,
And bled for Adam's helpless race:
'Tis mercy all, immense and free,
For, O my God, it found out me!

4 Long my imprisoned spirit lay
Fast bound in sin and nature's night;
Thine eye diffused a quickening ray,
I woke, the dungeon flamed with light;
My chains fell off, my heart was free,
I rose, went forth, and followed thee.

5 No condemnation now I dread,
Jesus, and all in him, is mine!
Alive in him, my living Head,
And clothed in righteousness divine,
Bold I approach the eternal throne,
And claim the crown, through Christ
my own.

This hymn was first published in "Hymns and Sacred Poems" in 1739. It describes Charles Wesley's own conversion. For two years after his return from Georgia in 1736, he battled with ill-health and doubts about his faith in God. After John returned in 1738, the brothers met Peter Böhler, who was in London for a few weeks on his way to missionary work in Carolina. Böhler convinced both Wesleys that they lacked "that faith whereby alone we are saved", but encouraged them to continue preaching: "Preach faith till you have it; and then, because you have it, you will preach faith". It proved to be a prophetic statement.

On Whit Sunday, 21st May 1738, Charles was very ill with pleurisy, and feared he might die. While reading his Bible, he heard a voice bidding him to arise and believe and he found himself at peace with God. On the following Wednesday, his brother John wrote in his diary, "I went very unwillingly to a society in Aldersgate Street . . ." There John found that same peace. Charles recounts, "Toward 10 my brother was brought in triumph . . . and declared 'I believe!' ".

Charles Wesley expresses his personal experience in this hymn, yet he is not introspective and does not dwell on his own feelings. Instead, he moves quickly from himself (v.1) to Christ (vv.2-3), so this hymn of praise can be sung by all Christians. The emphasis in the first verse on "for me" reflects Luther's commentary on the Epistle to the Galatians which Charles was reading at the time of his conversion. We read in his journal (17th May 1738) "Today I first saw Luther on the Galatians . . . I spent some hours this evening in private with Martin Luther, who was greatly blessed to me, especially his conclusion of the second chapter. I laboured, waited, and prayed to feel 'Who loved *me*, and gave Himself *for me*.' ". Luther had written, "Use thyself to lay hold of this little word *me* with a sure faith and apply it to thyself, and do not doubt that thou art of the number named in this little word *me*".

In v.2, Wesley recognizes that our faith is based on a "mystery" — the work of God baffles logic: "Great is the mystery of godliness" (*1 Timothy 3:16*). He points out the "impossible" combination of immortality and death (v.2.1)—yet it happened at Calvary. God's ways are beyond finding out—even by angels (v.2.3-4), so Wesley exhorts both angels and men to accept and adore (v.2.5-6).

Verse 3 summarizes Christ's life and death, from his incarnation (v.3.1-3) to the cross (v.3.4). In quoting *Philippians 2:7*, Charles, the classical scholar, goes back to the original Greek. "Emptied himself" (v.3.3) is much more accurate than the Authorized Version current in his day and anticipates the 1881 Revised Version, "Christ Jesus . . . emptied himself, taking the form of a servant . . .". The verse ends in praise, and returns to Wesley's personal experience: "it found out me!" (v.3.6). This naturally leads on to his own conversion experience, which is related opposite. Charles Wesley retells it in terms of Peter's experience of release from prison in Jerusalem, told in *Acts 12:5-11*. It is a story worth reading alongside v.4 of this hymn, for it shows Wesley's remarkable ability to put himself in the place of a character in the Bible and spiritualize the event. "Quickening ray" (v.4.3) means "life-giving"—hence the words in the next verse, "Alive in him" (v.5.3). This impressive phrase was probably borrowed from a poem by Pope, much of whose poetry Wesley knew by heart. In "Eloisa to Abelard" are the lines:

"Thy eyes diffused a reconciling ray
And gleams of glory brightened all the day."

The final verse brings the hymn to a fitting climax. Gone is the striving for acceptance by God described in Hymn 3 (page 10). Fear is replaced by peace and boldness. Faith is firmly based on the biblical revelation, so that this final verse becomes a marvellous mosaic of Scripture:-

5.1 (*Rom. 8:1*) 5.2 (*1 Cor. 1:30*) 5.3 (*Rom. 6:11*)
5.4 (*Isa. 61:10*) 5.5 (*Heb. 4:16*) 5.6 (*2 Tim. 4:8*)

O FOR A THOUSAND TONGUES TO SING MY GREAT REDEEMER'S PRAISE!

". . . thousands of thousands, saying with a loud voice 'Worthy is the Lamb that was slain, to receive power and riches and wisdom and strength and honour and glory and blessing'" (*Revelation 5:11-12*)

---

1 O for a thousand tongues to sing
My great Redeemer's praise,
The glories of my God and King,
The triumphs of his grace!

2 My gracious Master and my God,
Assist me to proclaim,
To spread through all the earth abroad
The honours of thy name.

3 Jesus! the name that charms our fears,
That bids our sorrows cease;
'Tis music in the sinner's ears,
'Tis life, and health, and peace.

4 He breaks the power of cancelled sin,
He sets the prisoner free;
His blood can make the foulest clean,
His blood availed for me.

5 He speaks, and, listening to his voice,
New life the dead receive,
The mournful, broken hearts rejoice,
The humble poor believe.

6 Hear him, ye deaf; his praise, ye dumb,
Your loosened tongues employ;
Ye blind, behold your Saviour come,
And leap, ye lame, for joy.

7 Look unto him, ye nations, own
Your God, ye fallen race;
Look, and be saved through faith alone,
Be justified by grace.

8 See all your sins on Jesus laid:
The Lamb of God was slain,
His soul was once an offering made
For every soul of man.

Charles Wesley entitled this hymn "For the Anniversary Day of One's Conversion". He wrote it in May 1739 to commemorate the first anniversary of his own conversion, and it was first published in "Hymns and Sacred Poems" 1740. The striking and memorable phrase "a thousand tongues" is often said to be based on a letter from Peter Böhler, the Moravian missionary who helped both Charles and John Wesley so much in the weeks before their conversions (see page 14). Böhler wrote, "Had I a thousand tongues, I would praise Him with them all". John Wesley placed this hymn first in his 1780 hymn book, and it retained that place in subsequent editions of "Wesley's Hymns" and its successor, "The Methodist Hymnbook". But after 203 years, the hymn was relegated to no. 744 in "Hymns and Psalms" (1983). However, the editors rediscovered an excellent concluding verse that had been omitted from the 1903 and 1933 editions. Originally, the verse began, 'With me, your chief . . .', but now it reads:-

'In Christ, our Head, you then shall know,/Shall feel, your sins forgiven,
Anticipate your heaven below,/And own that love is heaven.'

Few people who sing this hymn today realize that the verse beginning 'O for a thousand tongues' was originally verse 7 of an 18-verse poem. The original first verse was:-

'Glory to God, and praise and love/Be ever, ever given,
By saints below and saints above,/The Church in earth and heaven.'

Whether or not the actual wording of the opening line was taken from Peter Böhler's letter, in view of the original opening of Wesley's poem with its references to "The Church in earth and heaven", he probably had the verses from *Revelation 5* (printed opposite) in mind as well. We praise God for his glories and also for his triumphs: triumphs both in the universe and in individual hearts.,

Praise to God (v.1) soon moves to prayer to God in v.2. The prayer is for God's help to spread the news of the glories and triumphs of "my great Redeemer". This verse may be a rephrasing of a prayer in *Acts 4:29*: "And now Lord . . . grant unto thy servants that with all boldness they may speak thy word."

The theme of praise returns in v.3, where the words of each line can be traced to biblical passages. "Fear not" is one of Jesus' most frequently recorded phrases in the Gospels—hence v.3.1. 'He bids our sorrows cease' (v.3.2) recalls the verse "Then were the disciples glad, when they saw the Lord" (*John 20:20*). The name 'Jesus' is 'music in the sinner's ears' (v.3.3) because the name literally means "Saviour". 'Life, and health, and peace' (v.3.4) are all found in Jesus' words, "Thy faith hath made thee whole: go in peace" (*Mark 5:34*).

Verse 4 speaks of strength: breaking the power of sin (v.4.1); freeing the prisoner (v.4.2). Wesley's hymns have been unjustly criticized for portraying a "gentle" Jesus. This verse conveys a very different impression. Jesus' words in the synagogue, quoting from *Isaiah 61:1* are part of the inspiration for this verse: "He hath sent me . . . to preach deliverance to the captives . . .". Wesley explains the spiritual application of the prophecy Jesus quoted—something the first apostles were slow to understand. When the imprisoned John the Baptist wondered if Jesus really were the Messiah, Jesus told his disciples: "The blind receive their sight, and the lame walk, the lepers are cleansed, and the deaf hear, the dead are raised up, and the poor have the gospel preached to them" (*Matthew 11:4-5*), thus reminding them that Isaiah's prophecy was being fulfilled. Christ's words are paraphrased in verses 5 and 6 of the hymn, where Wesley again interprets them spiritually. From here the vision moves again to the whole world (v.7), expanding the prayer of v.2. The source is another passage from Isaiah: "Look unto me, and be ye saved, all the ends of the earth: for I am God, and there is none else" (*Isaiah 45:22*). But to this is added the New Testament theme, of salvation through faith alone, and justification by grace (v.7.3-4). The words may have been inspired by St. Augustine's phrase "Sola gratia; sola fide": "By grace alone; by faith alone".

Verse 8 expands the truths of v.7. 'Your sins' (v.8.1) can be interpreted personally, locally, or globally: personal salvation is linked with the vision of preaching to the whole world. The words refer to *Isaiah 53:5-12*: "The Lord hath laid on him the iniquity of us all . . . thou shalt make his soul an offering for sin . . . he bare the sin of many." Characteristically, Wesley emphasizes "*all* sins" (v.8.1) and "*every* soul"—the great ministry which both Charles and John Wesley exercised from their conversion until their deaths was preaching personal salvation through faith in Christ, for all people everywhere.

LET EARTH AND HEAVEN COMBINE

"Immanuel, God with us"

(*Matthew 1:23*)

1 Let earth and heaven combine,
  Angels and men agree,
To praise in songs divine
  The incarnate Deity,
Our God contracted to a span,
Incomprehensibly made man.

2 He laid his glory by,
  He wrapped him in our clay;
Unmarked by human eye,
  The latent Godhead lay;
Infant of days he here became,
And bore the mild Immanuel's name.

3 Unsearchable the love
  That hath the Saviour brought;
The grace is far above
  Or man or angel's thought;
Suffice for us that God, we know,
Our God, is manifest below.

4 He deigns in flesh to appear,
  Widest extremes to join;
To bring our vileness near,
  And make us all divine:
And we the life of God shall know,
For God is manifest below.

5 Made perfect first in love,
  And sanctified by grace,
We shall from earth remove,
  And see his glorious face:
Then shall his love be fully showed,
And man shall then be lost in God.

This hymn was first published in 1745 in "Hymns for the Nativity of our Lord" under the heading "Christmas". Wesley's best-known hymn on the Incarnation is, of course, "Hark the Herald Angels sing" (even though the first line is not his!). But he wrote several other fine hymns on the same theme, for example "Stupendous Height of Heavenly Love" and "To us a Child of Royal Birth". The hymn on this page deserves to be much better known. It can be sung throughout the year, even though it is especially suited to Christmastide.

Originally, there were six verses. Verse three read:

'See in that Infant's face
  The depth of Deity,
And labour while ye gaze
  To sound the mystery:
In vain; ye angels, gaze no more
  But fall, and silently adore.'

Throughout this hymn we praise "the Incarnate Deity" (v.1.4): the coming of God as Man is an incomprehensible miracle, and the basis of our Christian faith. Lesser poets would avoid the long word "incomprehensibly" in a short line of a hymn (v.1.6), but Wesley uses the word to emphasize the miracle of the incarnation. The previous phrase, "contracted to a span", is one he used elsewhere in his hymns to express the profound concept that God, who is beyond time, comes into human history at a specific time. The phrase has been traced to a poem by George Herbert, who was much admired by the Wesleys. Thus earth and heaven (v.1.1), angels and men (v.1.2) combine to sing praise to God: the angel songs at Bethlehem combined with the songs of Mary and Simeon at the time of Jesus' birth. Wherever Christians may be, their hymns of praise combine with the praise of angels to glorify the God who was incarnate at Bethlehem.

Verse 2 continues to reflect on the contrasts in the incarnation. His glory (v.2.1) becomes "wrapped in clay" (v.2.2). The "Ancient of Days" (*Daniel 7:9*) becomes the "Infant of Days" (v.2.5). The phrase "latent Godhead" (v.2.4) for the baby in a manger can be traced to "Latens Deitas" in the great hymn of St. Thomas Aquinas "Adoro te" ("I adore thee")—a hymn found in the Roman breviary. This may seem an unlikely source for Charles Wesley, but in 1747 he recorded that in Dublin "I spoke with great freedom . . . from the authority of their own Aquinas, and their own liturgy", so he must have known Aquinas' hymn well.

Verse 3 returns to the theme that the full meaning of the Incarnation is far above and beyond our understanding—or even "angel thought". Overwhelmed by this, we are encouraged by the last couplet of the verse: we do not need to understand fully, nor can we. We are called to believe the fundamental fact that in the incarnation (v.3.5-6) "God was manifest in the flesh" (*1 Timothy 3:16*).

The Incarnation joins "widest extremes" (v.4.2): God becomes flesh (v.4.1), and sinners can approach the sinless God (v.4.3). We can take on something of the divine nature (v.4.4) and shall come to know the life of God (v.4.5). In St. John's great statement about the incarnation we read of "the Word" that "in him was life" (*John 1.4)*, and later Jesus said, "I am come that they might have life, and that they might have it more abundantly" (*John 10:10*). Thus we thank God for our new life (v.5.1), for his grace that has sanctified us (v.5.2), and for the expectation of future life in his presence, when we "shall see his face" (*Revelation 22:4;* v.5.4). The hymn starts with eternity "contracted to a span", and ends with eternity: "man shall then be lost in God" (v.5.6).

O LOVE DIVINE! WHAT HAST THOU DONE?

"And about the ninth hour Jesus cried with a loud voice . . . My God, my God, why hast thou forsaken me? . . . when he had cried again with a loud voice (he) yielded up the ghost."
(*Matthew 27:46, 50*)

---

1 O Love Divine! what hast thou done?
The immortal God hath died for me.
The Father's co-eternal Son
Bore all my sins upon the tree;
The immortal God for me hath died,
My Lord, my Love is crucified.

2 Behold him, all ye that pass by,
The bleeding Prince of life and peace
Come, see, ye worms, your Maker die,
And say, was ever grief like his?
Come, feel with me his blood applied:
My Lord, my Love is crucified.

3 Is crucified for me and you,
To bring us rebels back to God:
Believe, believe the record true,
Ye all are bought with Jesu's blood,
Pardon for all flows from his side;
My Lord, my Love is crucified.

4 Then let us sit beneath his cross,
And gladly catch the healing stream,
All things for him account but loss,
And give up all our hearts to him;
Of nothing think or speak beside,
"My Lord, my Love is crucified."

This hymn was first published in 1742 in "Hymns and Sacred poems" in the section for Passiontide. The most striking feature is the refrain, "My Lord, my Love is crucified." at the end of each verse. It is found in the Epistle to the Romans written by St. Ignatius (died c.107), one of the Apostolic Fathers: "For my love has been crucified and there is left in me no fire of earthly love at all." The Wesleys knew the writings of St. Ignatius well. Their father, Samuel Wesley (Sr.) wrote in a letter of advice to a young clergyman, "The blessed Ignatius's Epistles can never be enough read, or praised, or valued, next to the inspired writings". This letter was later published by John, who also included writings by St. Ignatius in his "Christian Library".

"My Lord, my Love was crucified" was the first line of a hymn by John Mason (c.1645-94) which was published in 1683, and can still be found in some hymnbooks today (e.g. the final hymn in "Christian Worship"). A century later, F. W. Faber (1814-63) used the phrase in a hymn he wrote on the crucifixion.

This meditation on the crucifixion of Christ begins with author and readers exclaiming in awe at this act of God (v.1.1). Jesus chose to die: "I lay down my life . . . No man taketh it from me, but I lay it down of myself" (*John 10:17-18*). Twice in the opening verse (v.1.2 and v.1.5) Wesley wonders at the contradiction that God, who is immortal (literally 'not subject to death') should choose to die. He never ceased to be amazed at this mystery, and expresses the paradox in a number of hymns (e.g. "And can it be . . .", p.14). To stress the divinity of the Christ who died, he asserts with the Athanasian Creed that Father and Son are co-eternal (v.1.3). It is God incarnate "who his own self bare our sins in his own body on the tree" (*1 Peter 2:24*).

Christ was crucified before a crowd: "they that passed by reviled him" (*Matthew 27:39;* v.2.1). Wesley reminds us with St. Peter that "ye denied the Holy One . . . and killed the Prince of life . . ." (*Acts 3:14-15*; v.2.2). He was "a man of sorrows and acquainted with grief" (*Isaiah 53:3*). "Is it nothing to you all ye that pass by? behold, and see if there be any sorrow like unto my sorrow . . ." (*Lamentations 1:12*) is the question asked in v.2.1 and v.2.4.

Verse 3 stresses the *purpose* of the crucifixion: "When we were enemies we were reconciled to God by the death of his Son" (*Romans 5:2;* v.3.2); "for ye are bought with a price" (*1 Corinthians 6:20*) and ". . . ye were not redeemed with corruptible things . . . but with the precious blood of Christ" (*1 Peter 1:18-19*; v.3.4). Then we return to the scene at the cross (v.3.5) where, after Jesus died, "one of the soliders with a spear pierced his side, and forthwith came there out blood and water . . ." (*John 19:34-35*). This is the scene which dominates the last verse. Wesley may have been thinking of medieval paintings which depict angels catching the blood which flows from the Saviour's side. He sees the blood and water as the means and symbol of forgiveness for "the blood of Jesus Christ his Son cleanseth us from all sin" (*1 John 1:7;* v.4.2).

If we 'believe the record true' (v.3.3), then the crucifixion demands a response. Wesley combines Paul's words (v.4.3-4) ". . . I count all things but loss for the excellency of the knowledge of Christ Jesus my Lord" (*Philippians 3:8*) and "That Christ may dwell in your hearts by faith" (*Ephesians 3:17*). That indwelling will control our thoughts and words (v.4.5) and lead us to acknowledge Christ's Lordship, Christ's love, and the power of his crucifixion (v.4.6).

CHRIST THE LORD IS RISEN TODAY

"And he saith unto them, Be not affrighted: Ye seek Jesus of Nazareth, which was crucified: he is risen: he is not here: behold the place where they laid him"

(*Mark 16:6*)

---

1 "Christ, the Lord, is risen to-day"
Sons of men and angels say!
Raise your joys and triumphs high:
Sing, ye heavens; thou earth, reply.

2 Love's redeeming work is done;
Fought the fight, the battle won:
Lo! the sun's eclipse is o'er,
Lo! he sets in blood no more!

3 Vain the stone, the watch, the seal,
Christ hath burst the gates of hell:
Death in vain forbids his rise,
Christ hath opened Paradise.

4 Lives again our glorious King!
Where, O death, is now thy sting?
Once he died, our souls to save;
Where's thy victory, boasting grave?

5 Soar we now where Christ hath led,
Following our exalted Head:
Made like him, like him we rise,
Ours the cross, the grave, the skies.

6 King of glory! Soul of bliss!
Everlasting life is this,
Thee to know, thy power to prove,
Thus to sing, and thus to love.

This hymn was first published in 1739 in "Hymns and Sacred Poems", with the title "Hymn for Easter Day". There were 11 verses, but five of these are almost always now omitted. Omitted from the 1780 hymnbook, the hymn was added in the 1831 supplement to "Wesley's Hymns". However, before 1780 it had appeared in several other hymnbooks, for example in Martin Madan's "Psalms and Hymns", 1760. Madan changed verse 4, line 3 from "Dying once, he all doth save" to "Once he died our souls to save"; this amendment is now in common use.

The most familiar tune to this hymn is called "Savannah", the name of the American town where John Wesley was chaplain. It is a Moravian tune, first printed in England by John Wesley in 1742 in his book "A Collection of Tunes set to Music, as they are commonly sung at the Foundery". The Foundery was his London meeting-house. In that book, he called the tune "Herrnhuth", after the Moravian settlement in Germany, but later he renamed it "Savannah".

"Christ the Lord is risen to-day!" is a joyful affirmation that Christians can sing both on Easter Day and on any day of the year. Angels and men (v.1.2); heaven and earth (v.1.4) join in the triumphant song. Perhaps because the first line is associated solely with Easter Day, some hymnbooks start this hymn with verse 2: Love's redeeming work is done;/Fought the fight, the battle won. This couplet is one of the simplest yet most profound statements of the meaning of the Crucifixion and Resurrection—the powers of evil were defeated on the Cross, and the victory proclaimed by the empty tomb. The 'sun's eclipse' (v.2.3) refers both to the darkness at the time of the Crucifixion (*Luke 23:44-45*), and to the death of the "Sun of Righteousness" (*Malachi 4:2*). In poetic language (v.2.4), the red of sunset is linked with the shed blood of Christ.

Verse 3 is closely modelled on a verse of a now forgotten hymn for Easter by Samuel Wesley, Charles' eldest brother: "In vain the stone, the watch, the seal [cf *Matthew 27:65*f]/Forbid an early rise/To Him who burst the bars of Hell/And opened Paradise." It expresses well men's pathetic efforts to contain Jesus the Son of God, who chose to die and rise again (*Acts 2:23-24*).

1 Corinthians 15 is Paul's great chapter on the meaning of the Resurrection, and Wesley uses the apostle's conclusion in v.4.2,4: "O death, where is thy sting?" "O grave, where is thy victory?"—words from *1 Corinthians 15:55*. These words appear in the 'Easter Anthem' in the Prayer Book, which Charles Wesley would have known well. Other lines in verses 3 and 4 can be traced to verses of *Romans 6* which are also in the Easter Anthem, the series of verses from Paul's Epistles normally sung on Easter Day.

Verse 5 refers to the Ascension, which was inseparable from the Resurrection for the Wesleys. The last line, 'Ours the cross, the grave, the skies' is now a phrase of triumph: Christ's victory has become our victory. This line contrasts with 'Vain the stone, the watch, the seal' (v.3.1): man's "victory" scarcely lasted three days—Christ's victory is eternal.

The opening of the final verse is said to have been borrowed from Young's "Last Day", published in 1713: Triumphant King of Glory! Soul of bliss!/What a stupendous turn of fate is this! "King of Glory" is a biblical title: "Who is this King of glory? The Lord strong and mighty" (*Psalm 24:8*). Everlasting life (v.6.2) is clearly seen as including present time. The source is Jesus' prayer, "This is life eternal, that they might know thee, the only true God, and Jesus Christ whom thou hast sent" (*John 17:3*). Thus (v.6.4), we sing praises both now and for ever: the hymn ends as it began, with praise to the risen Christ.

HAIL THE DAY THAT SEES HIM RISE

"And it came to pass, while he blessed them, he was parted from them, and carried up into heaven. And they worshipped him . . ." (*Luke 24: 51-52*).

---

1 Hail the day that sees him rise, Alleluya!
To his throne above the skies; Alleluya!
Christ, awhile to mortals given, Alleluya!
Enters now the highest heaven! Alleluya!

2 There the glorious triumph waits;
Lift your heads, eternal gates!
Christ hath conquered death and sin;
Take the King of glory in.

3 See! the heaven its Lord receives,
Yet he loves the earth he leaves:
Though returning to his throne,
Still he calls mankind his own.

4 See! he lifts his hands above;
See! he shows the prints of love:
Hark! his gracious lips bestow
Blessings on his Church below.

5 Still for us he intercedes;
His prevailing death he pleads;
Near himself prepares our place,
He the first-fruits of our race.

6 Lord, though parted from our sight,
Far above yon azure height,
Grant our hearts may thither rise,
Seeking thee beyond the skies.

7 There we shall with thee remain,
Partners of thine endless reign;
There thy face unclouded see,
Find our heaven of heavens in thee.

In the introduction to his 1780 hymnbook, John Wesley wrote, "Many gentlemen have done my brother and me . . . the honour to reprint many of our hymns. Now they are perfectly welcome to do so, provided they print them just as they are. But I desire they would not attempt to mend them; for they really are not able . . .". Often "improvements" are later seen to be less good than the original: in the case of this hymn, however, the popularity of the revision seems well justified. For although this is one of the best-known of all Charles Wesley's hymns, it is most usually sung in this revision of Wesley's original. His "Hymn for Ascension Day" was first published with this title in "Hymns and Sacred Poems", 1739. It was not included in the 1780 hymnbook, but was added in later supplements. The present Methodist Hymn Book has six of Wesley's original 10 verses, but few other books print Wesley's words. The majority of hymnbooks today use this version, amended by T. Cotterill.

In 1820, Thomas Cotterill, the curate of St. Paul's Church, Sheffield, published his "Selection of Psalms and Hymns", including his own amended form of this hymn. The amendments are numerous, but mostly minor, so Charles Wesley is rightly described as the author. Later editors have made other minor amendments, and in 1852 the "Alleluias" were first added. The addition of the refrain has usually resulted in fewer verses being sung, and verses 3, 7 and 9 of the original are normally omitted now, as here.

For Christians, the Ascension is Christ's triumph. It marks his victorious return to God's throne in heaven. And this triumphant hymn is perhaps the best-known of all that handle the theme. For many years, the BBC has broadcast the first verse immediately before the 8 a.m. news on Ascension Day: no other hymn could be considered for that occasion.

Verse 1 summarises the theology of Ascension Day. It is a day of joy (v.1.1), when Christ returned to the throne that is his by right (v.1.2) after a few years of human life (v.1.3). It is to highest heaven that he returns (v.1.4)—a phrase from Solomon's prayer at the dedication of the first temple (*1 Kings 8:27*).

In v.2 the scene is recounted in terms of Psalm 24, which is associated with Ascension Day in Christian liturgy. "Lift up your heads, O ye gates, and be ye lift up, ye everlasting doors, and the King of Glory shall come in" (v.2.2, 4; *Psalm 24:7*). Cotterill has added (v.2.3) another clear statement of the form of Christ's victory—a much more positive line than Wesley's original ("Wide unfold the radiant scene").

Verse 3 stresses that the Ascension to heaven was not the desertion of earth. As Jesus promised, the Apostles discovered this at Pentecost. Before Jesus ascended, "he led them out as far as to Bethany, and he lifted up his hands, and he blessed them" (*Luke 24:50*). The hands outstretched to bless showed the wounds of the crucifixion (v.4.1-2). His death is still the source of blessing for his church (v.4.4) and the means of our access to God (v.5.2). "He is able also to save them to the uttermost that come unto God by him, seeing he ever liveth to make intercession for them" (v.5.1, 2; *Hebrews 7:25*)—Christ is both our High Priest and our sacrificed Lamb in heaven. He prepares for our arrival: "In my Father's house are many mansions: . . . I go to prepare a place for you" (v.5.3; *John 14:2*). And he shows us the way through death: "For as in Adam all die, even so in Christ shall all be made alive . . . Christ the firstfruits . . ." (v.5.4; *1 Corinthians 15:23*).

The last two verses are a prayer, very closely based on the ancient collect for Ascension Day: "Grant, we beseech thee, Almighty God, that like as we do believe thy only-begotten Son our Lord Jesus Christ to have ascended into the heavens (v.6.1, 2); so we may also in heart and mind thither ascend (v.6.3, 4), and with him continually dwell (v.7.1), who liveth, and reigneth with thee and the Holy Ghost, one God, world without end (v.7.2). Amen." Many of Wesley's hymns look forward to heaven, when "shall we ever be with the Lord" (v.7.1; *1 Thessalonians 4:17*). There is the vision of the future (v.7.2, 3; *Revelation 22:4, 5*), but eternal life begins now. The final line refers to a possibility for the present, not merely a hope for the future—that we "Find our heaven of heavens in Thee".

COME, HOLY GHOST, OUR HEARTS INSPIRE

"Holy men of God spake as they were moved by the Holy Ghost" *(2 Peter 1:21)*

---

1 Come, Holy Ghost, our hearts inspire,
Let us thine influence prove,
Source of the old prophetic fire,
Fountain of light and love.

2 Come, Holy Ghost (for moved by thee
The prophets wrote and spoke),
Unlock the truth, thyself the key,
Unseal the sacred book.

3 Expand thy wings, celestial Dove,
Brood o'er our nature's night;
On our disordered spirits move,
And let there now be light.

4 God, through himself, we then shall know
If thou within us shine,
And sound, with all thy saints below,
The depths of love divine.

This hymn was first published in "Hymns and Sacred Poems" in 1740. The heading in 1740, and in "Wesley's Hymns" is "Before reading the Scriptures", but the hymn can clearly be used in other contexts too. The first part of the hymn shows some similarities with "Veni Creator Spiritus", the medieval poem which is the only hymn in the Church of England Prayer Book (see "Come Holy Ghost our souls inspire" in the companion volume 'Praise with Understanding'.) However, Wesley's hymn is not another translation, but an original composition which owes its inspiration mainly to biblical passages.

Verse 1 prays for the inspiration (literally the "breathing in") of the Holy Ghost in our hearts. On the first Easter Day, Jesus "breathed on the disciples, and saith unto them, Receive ye the Holy Ghost" (*John 20:22*). Thus we too pray for inspiration. The Holy Ghost is described as both 'fire' (v.1.3) and 'fountain' (v.1.4): neither is a fully adequate description, but both words are helpful in interpreting the Spirit's purpose. Wesley looks back to the work of the prophets (v.1.3) and speaks of the present too (v.1.4). 'Fountain of light and love' reminds us that the Spirit imparts God's nature: "God is light" (*1 John 1:5*) and "God is love" (*1 John 4:8*).

Verse 2 asks the Holy Ghost to come now as in the past, "For prophecy came not in old time by the will of man: but holy men of God spake as they were moved by the Holy Ghost" (*2 Peter 1:21*). We pray that he will unlock and unseal—'Thyself the key' (v.2.3) is a memorable phrase—for as the inspirer of Scripture he alone can be its interpreter. "When the Spirit of truth is come, he will lead you into all truth" is Christ's promise (*John 16:13*).

With v.3 we move further back in time, to creation and the first chapter of Genesis. Charles Wesley had an unparalleled ability to link widely-separated passages of the Bible: he was a living example of the Holy Spirit unlocking the truth from the sacred book. A century later, the same passage was used in the well-known hymn "Thou whose Almighty Word": it may be that this hymn inspired the later one.

Wesley relates *Genesis 1:1-3* to *us*. "Darkness was upon the face of the deep" becomes '*Our* nature's night' (v.3.2). "The earth was without form and void" becomes '*our* disordered spirits' (v.3.3). "Let there be light" appears in both Bible and hymn (v.3.4). In the Bible, God speaks the words, and the sentence ends "and there was light"; in the hymn they express our prayer for light now. The prayer is answered: 'If thou (the Holy Ghost) within us shine' (v.4.2). The light is the light of the knowledge of God (v.4.1). Furthermore, we can 'sound the depths of love divine' (v.4.3-4) for "God hath revealed them unto us by his Spirit: for the Spirit searcheth all things, yea, the deep things of God" (*1 Corinthians 2:9-10*). We cannot fully know God, but *we can* 'sound the depths' through God the Holy Spirit.

LO! HE COMES WITH CLOUDS DESCENDING

"Every eye shall see him"

(*Revelation 1:7*)

1 Lo! He comes with clouds descending,
Once for favoured sinners slain;
Thousand thousand saints attending,
Swell the triumph of his train:
Hallelujah!
God appears on earth to reign.

2 Every eye shall now behold him
Robed in dreadful majesty;
Those who set at nought and sold him,
Pierced and nailed him to the tree,
Deeply wailing,
Shall the true Messiah see.

3 The dear tokens of his passion
Still his dazzling body bears;
Cause of endless exultation
To his ransomed worshippers;
With what rapture
Gaze we on those glorious scars!

4 Yea, Amen! let all adore thee,
High on thy eternal throne;
Saviour, take the power and glory,
Claim the kingdom for thine own;
Hallelujah!
Everlasting God, come down!

This hymn was first published by Charles Wesley in "Hymns of Intercession for all Mankind" in 1758. However, a hymn on the same theme and in the same metre had previously been written and published in Dublin by John Cennick in 1752: 'Lo he cometh, countless trumpets" . . . : Wesley knew of this when he wrote his own, much finer hymn.

Martin Madan, in his "Collection of Psalms and Hymns", 1762, combined parts of Cennick's hymn with Wesley's, and this version was popular for a time, but most hymnbooks now use Wesley's original hymn, sometimes with small alterations from Madan.

This hymn about the return of Christ in triumph to reign draws together various parts of the vision of John recorded in the book of Revelation. The Second Coming of Jesus is set vividly in the present tense: "Behold, he *cometh* with clouds" (v.1.1; *Revelation 1:7*). 'Thousand, thousand saints attending' (v.1.3) is based on a later chapter: "I heard the voice of many angels round the throne . . . and the number of them was ten thousand times ten thousand, and thousands of thousands" (*Revelation 5:11*). The Christ who returns is both Saviour (v.1.2) and God (v.1.6). He is fulfilling the prophecy of the angels at his Ascension: "This same Jesus, which is taken up from you into heaven, shall so come in like manner as ye have seen him go into heaven" (*Acts 1:11*). Jesus left a few disciples gazing upwards as he ascended: he returns in triumph to the whole world (v.2.1), as Judge (v.2) as well as Saviour (v.3). Verse 2 paraphrases the second part of *Revelation 1:7*, " . . . every eye shall see him, and they also which pierced him: and all kindreds of the earth shall wail because of him".

The wailing of v.2 contrasts with the worship of v.3. The wounds of Jesus, which provided the proof of his resurrection to "doubting Thomas", now symbolize the ascended Christ's continuing humanity and saving love. The thousands of *Revelation 5:11* are "saying with a loud voice, Worthy is the Lamb *that was slain* to receive power and riches and wisdom and strength and honour and glory and blessing" (*Revelation 5:12*), and we shall join the exultation of those he ransomed (v.3.3-4).

Thus we can call on everyone (v.4.1) to adore the 'true Messiah'. 'Yea, Amen' (meaning 'Yes indeed') brings us back yet again to *Revelation 1:7*, which concludes "Even so, Amen". We have here the fulfilment of the words of the Lord's prayer, "Thy kingdom come . . . for thine is the kingdom, and the power and the glory, for ever and ever" (v.4.3, 4). The hymn concludes with the final prayer of the Bible, "Even so come, Lord Jesus" (v.4.6; *Revelation 22:20*).

The hymn thus expresses both the solemnity and the joy of the Second Coming. In churches which observe Advent it is often confined to the pre-Christmas season, but it is in fact a hymn which can be appropriately sung at any time of the year.

CHRIST WHOSE GLORY FILLS THE SKIES

"That was the true Light, which lighteth every man that cometh into the world" (*John 1:9*)

1 Christ, whose glory fills the skies,
  Christ, the true, the only Light,
Sun of righteousness arise,
  Triumph o'er the shades of night;
Day-spring from on high, be near;
Day-star, in my heart appear!

2 Dark and cheerless is the morn,
  Unaccompanied by thee:
Joyless is the day's return,
  Till thy mercy's beams I see;
Till thou inward light impart.
Glad my eyes, and warm my heart.

3 Visit then this soul of mine,
  Pierce the gloom of sin and grief;
Fill me, Radiancy Divine!
  Scatter all my unbelief:
More and more thyself display,
Shining to the perfect day!

This hymn was first published under the heading "A Morning Hymn" in "Hymns and Sacred Poems" in 1740. It was not included in Wesley's 1780 Hymnbook, because there was no section for "Morning Hymns" or, indeed, for hymns for any other special times, days or occasions. In fact, it was not until 1875 that this hymn was included in "Wesley's Hymns". It is now found in almost all hymnbooks. Charles Wesley used the same first line for another hymn, which was included in the 1780 book, but is little known now:

Christ whose glory fills the skies,
  That famous Plant thou art,
Tree of life eternal, rise
  In every longing heart.

This is one of several hymns referred to in George Eliot's "Adam Bede". Seth Bede, the village Methodist, repeats it as he walks home. The hymnwriter James Montgomery regarded it as one of the finest of Charles Wesley's hymns.

This "morning hymn" has light as its theme: the light is Christ, "the true Light" (*John 1:9;* v.1.2). The hymn starts with a magnificent vision of the universe. Then follows a picture of sunrise on earth (v.1.3-5)—of the "dayspring", a much more vivid word than "dawn". There are only two references in all the Bible to Christ as sun and as dayspring, and Wesley links these together. "Unto you that fear my name shall the Sun of Righteousness arise, with healing in his wings" (v.1.3). This comes from *Malachi 4:2,* on the last page of the Old Testament—and the source for lines in another Wesley hymn, "Hark the Herald Angels sing". The opening chapter of Luke's gospel contains the words of Zecharias, John the Baptist's father: "The Dayspring from on high hath visited us" (*Luke 1:78;* v.1.5). The last line of v.1 moves to "my heart"—in six short lines the scale has changed from the incomprehensibly vast and most distant to the smallest and closest. Once again, the imagery is entirely biblical: ". . . take heed, as unto a light that shineth in a dark place, until the day dawn, and the day star arise in your hearts" (*2 Peter 1:19*). This 'day star' is the 'Sun of Righteousness'.

In contrast to the glory of the sunrise of Christ's presence in v.1, v.2 describes a sunless dawn. Just as dawn without the sun is 'cheerless' (v.2.1), so life without Christ's inward light is joyless (v.2.3). The concept of Christ as the Sun is maintained. As the beams of the sun are the source of light and heat, so the beams of Christ's mercy are the source of inward light and warmth (v.2.4-6).

Verse 3 then offers a resolution of the contrasts of the sunrise of v.1 and the sunless dawn of v.2, with a prayer for Christ to visit us (v.3.1), to fill us (v.3.3), and to reveal himself to us more and more (v.3.5). Only his light can pierce our 'gloom of sin' (v.3.2). As the rising sun evaporates the mists from the ground, so we pray for Christ to remove our unbelief (v.3.4): "Lord I believe, help thou my unbelief" (*Mark 9:24*). Finally, the vision is of "the perfect day" (v.3.6). "The path of the just is as the shining light, that shineth more and more unto the perfect day" (*Proverbs 4:18*). For those made just by Christ, this anticipates heaven: "The city had no need of the sun . . . for the glory of God did lighten it, and the Lamb is the light thereof" (*Revelation 21:23*). Thus the last line of the hymn returns to the theme of the first line: 'Christ, whose glory fills the skies'.

COME, O THOU TRAVELLER UNKNOWN

"And Jacob was left alone; and there wrestled a man with him until the breaking of the day" (*Genesis 32:24*)

---

1 Come, O thou Traveller unknown,
Whom still I hold, but cannot see!
My company before is gone,
And I am left alone with thee;
With thee all night I mean to stay,
And wrestle till the break of day.

2 I need not tell thee who I am,
My misery and sin declare;
Thyself hast called me by my name,
Look on thy hands and read it there;
But who, I ask thee, who art Thou?
Tell me Thy name, and tell me now.

3 In vain thou strugglest to get free,
I never will unloose my hold!
Art thou the Man that died for me?
The secret of thy love unfold;
Wrestling, I will not let thee go,
Till I thy name, thy nature know.

4 Wilt thou not yet to me reveal
Thy new, unutterable name?
Tell me, I still beseech thee, tell;
To know it now resolved I am;
Wrestling, I will not let thee go,
Till I thy name, thy nature know.

5 What though my shrinking flesh complain,
And murmur to contend so long?
I rise superior to my pain,
When I am weak, then I am strong;
And when my all of strength shall fail,
I shall with the God-man prevail.

6 Yield to me now, for I am weak,
But confident in self-despair;
Speak to my heart, in blessings speak,
Be conquered by my instant prayer;
Speak, or thou never hence shalt move,
And tell me if thy name is Love.

7 'Tis Love! 'tis Love! thou diedst for me!
I hear thy whisper in my heart;
The morning breaks, the shadows flee,
Pure, universal love thou art;
To me, to all, thy bowels move,
Thy nature and thy name is Love.

8 My prayer hath power with God; the grace
Unspeakable I now receive;
Through faith I see thee face to face,
I see thee face to face, and live!
In vain I have not wept and strove;
Thy nature and thy name is Love.

9 I know thee, Saviour, who thou art,
Jesus, the feeble sinner's friend;
Nor wilt thou with the night depart,
But stay and love me to the end,
Thy mercies never shall remove;
Thy nature and thy name is Love.

10 The Sun of righteousness on me
Hath rose with healing in his wings,
Withered my nature's strength; from thee
My soul its life and succour brings;
My help is all laid up above;
Thy nature and thy name is Love.

11 Contented now upon my thigh
I halt, till life's short journey end;
All helplessness, all weakness I
On thee alone for strength depend,
Nor have I power from thee to move;
Thy nature and thy name is Love.

12 Lame as I am, I take the prey,
Hell, earth, and sin, with ease o'ercome;
I leap for joy, pursue my way,
And as a bounding hart fly home,
Through all eternity to prove
Thy nature and thy name is Love.

Isaac Watts said, "That single poem, 'Wrestling Jacob', is worth all the verses I myself have written." Charles Wesley probably intended it to remain as a poem, but its original 14 verses were included in his brother John's 1742 "Hymns and Sacred Poems".

Charles Wesley used the story of Jacob wrestling with the Angel of the Lord (*Genesis 32:24-32*) to tell of his own spiritual conversion. It is one of several long poems where he took a Bible story, and rewrote events from the point of view of his own Christian experience.

Jacob is returning home with his family, servants, flocks and wealth and is about to meet his brother Esau, who he fears may take revenge. He has sent his "company" ahead, spending the night by himself to seek God's support (v.1.3,4; *Genesis 32:9-12; 21-24*). In the darkness "there wrestled a man with him" (v.1.1, 2; 5, 6; *Genesis 32:24*). Unable to overcome Jacob, he puts Jacob's thigh out of joint (*Genesis 32:25*; v.5.1-3). Jacob will not give in, and at dawn the man begs to go, but Jacob demands a blessing before releasing him (*Genesis 32:26*; vv.3; 4.5, 6; 6). The man asks Jacob's name, which meant "supplanter" and well described much of his life (*Genesis 32:27* and *27:36*; v.2.1-4). The stranger gives Jacob a new name, "Israel", "for as a prince hast thou power with God and with men and hast prevailed" (*Genesis 32:28*), and this prompts Jacob to demand the stranger's name. Jacob receives no direct answer, but he does receive a blessing and realizes that his contender was none other than God himself in human form: "I have seen God face to face, and my life is preserved" (*Genesis 32: 29-30;* the key to v.2.5, 6; 3.3-6; 4-10). Already the contender has gone; As the sun rises Jacob is left to limp towards Esau (*Genesis 32: 31-32;* vv.11, 12).

The only place in the Bible where this story is mentioned again is in *Hosea 12:4, 5*: "Jacob . . . had power over the angel and prevailed: he wept, and made supplication unto him . . . Even the Lord God of Hosts . . .". Commentators have long recognized that "the Angel (Messenger) of the Lord" who appears in several Old Testament passages is God himself in human form—a paradox which becomes meaningful with the New Testament revelation of the pre-existent Son (*John 8:58*). Thus Wesley recognizes Jacob's opponent as "the Man that died for me" (v.3.3), i.e. the crucified Christ. Thus he puts himself with his sin (v.2.1-4) in Jacob's place, and wrestles in prayer (v.6.4) with Christ until the "God-Man" (v.5.6) will reveal his new name and nature (v.3.6; 4). As with Jacob, there is no announcement, but a dawning in the heart: "And tell me if thy name is Love./'Tis Love! 'tis love! Thou diedst for me!" (v.6.6-7.1).

Wesley weaves many New Testament ideas in with the Genesis passage. The weakened Jacob prevailing with the stranger (v.5.4) aptly illustrates *2 Corinthians 12:10* "When I am weak, then am I strong." "Hereby perceive we the love of God, because he laid down his life for us" (*1 John 3:16*) and "God is love" (*1 John 4:8*) are the key to 'Thy nature and thy name is Love' (v.7 and the final line of all succeeding verses). Wesley contrasts the 'God-Man's' departure at sunrise with the permanent presence of Christ with the Christian. The thought of sunrise evokes *Malachi 4:2* (v.10.1-2) and contrasts God's strength and healing with his weakness. God made Jacob lame, yet named him 'Israel', a powerful prince (v.10.3-6; 11). When Isaiah looked forward to the Messianic age he promised, "The lame take the prey" and "Then shall the lame man leap as a hart . . ." (*Isaiah 33:23; 35:6*; v.12.1; 3-4). With this thought Wesley anticipates having 'all eternity to prove/Thy nature and Thy name is love'.

COMMIT THOU ALL THY GRIEFS

"In all thy ways acknowledge him, and he shall direct thy paths" (*Proverbs 3:6*)

---

1 Commit thou all thy griefs
And ways into his hands,
To his sure truth and tender care,
Who heaven and earth commands.

2 Who points the clouds their course,
Whom winds and seas obey,
He shall direct thy wandering feet,
He shall prepare thy way.

3 Thou on the Lord rely,
So safe shalt thou go on;
Fix on his work thy steadfast eye,
So shall thy work be done.

4 No profit canst thou gain
By self-consuming care;
To him commend thy cause, his ear
Attends the softest prayer.

5 Thy everlasting truth,
Father, thy ceaseless love,
Sees all thy children's wants, and knows
What best for each will prove.

6 Thou everywhere hast sway,
And all things serve thy might;
Thy every act pure blessing is,
Thy path unsullied light.

7 Give to the winds thy fears;
Hope, and be undismayed;
God hears thy sighs, and counts thy tears,
God shall lift up thy head.

8 Through waves, and clouds, and storms,
He gently clears thy way:
Wait thou his time, so shall this night
Soon end in joyous day.

9 Leave to his sovereign sway
To choose and to command;
So shalt thou wondering own his way,
How wise, how strong his hand.

10 Far, far above thy thought
His counsel shall appear,
When fully he the work hath wrought
That caused thy needless fear!

11 Thou seest our weakness, Lord;
Our hearts are known to thee;
O lift thou up the sinking hand,
Confirm the feeble knee!

12 Let us in life, in death,
Thy steadfast truth declare,
And publish with our latest breath
Thy love and guardian care.

This hymn is a free translation by John Wesley of the great German hymn *"Befiehl du deine Wege"* by Paul Gerhardt (1607-1676). The original was first published in 1653 in Cruger's "Praxis Pietatis Melica", so is nearly a century older than Wesley's hymn, which appeared in 1739. The German hymn was an acrostic on Luther's version of Psalm 37. It had 12 verses of eight lines, and was designed for use in sections during a service. Wesley reduced its length by a third, and several of his verses are normally now omitted—indeed, many hymn-books give fewer verses than here. In "Wesley's Hymns", his version is in two parts and is entitled "Trust in Providence". Some hymnbooks have separated the two parts, so that "Give to the winds thy fears" (v.7.1) becomes an opening line.

The great length of the hymn, and its reference to 'griefs' at the beginning has possibly make it less well known that it deserves to be. Several hymnbooks use a briefer form, much amended by an unknown person, which was first published in 1836 and begins with the fine verse:

Put thou thy trust in God,/In duty's path go on.
Walk in his strength with faith and hope,/So shall thy work be done.

In his grief, Job was told "I would seek unto God, and unto God would I commit my cause, which doeth great things and unsearchable" (*Job 5:8-9*). This text may be the inspiration for v.1 and for the theme of the whole hymn. The same thought can be found in the New Testament: "Casting all your care upon him, for he careth for you" (*1 Peter 5:7*).

Verse 2 speaks of God's work in nature. Job was shown the greatness of God in nature, and from this deduced that God was able to cope with human crises, too: "Can any understand the spreading of the clouds?" (v.2.1; *Job. 36:29*). The disciples of Jesus, too, marvelled at Christ's power over nature: "What manner of man is this, that even the winds and sea obey him!" (*Matthew 8:27*). By thinking of God's work, we will accomplish our work, if we rely on him (v.3). The answer to grief is not worry—'self-consuming care' (v.4.1, 2)—but prayer to God (v.4.3, 4): "Fret not thyself . . . Commit thy way unto the Lord; trust also in him" (*Psalm 37: 1-5*).

Verses 5 and 6 return to the theme of God's unchanging and unchangeable goodness, love and power: "My God shall supply all your need by Christ Jesus" (*Philippians 4:19*) is a key thought here.

Part 2 of the hymn deals more specifically with sorrow. Verse 7 reflects on *Psalm 42:5*, "Why art thou cast down, O my soul, and why art thou disquieted within me? Hope thou in God, for I shall yet praise him". Clouds and storms (v.8) seem to threaten us, but we have already sung (v.2) that the clouds and winds are in God's hands. We also have another verse of a Psalm to encourage us: "They cry unto the Lord in their trouble, and he bringeth them out of their distress. He maketh the storm a calm, so that the waves thereof are still" (*Psalm 107:28-29*). The waiting-time (v.8.3) tries our patience, but "The Lord is good unto them that wait for him . . . it is good that a man should both hope and quietly wait for the salvation of the Lord" (*Lamentations 3:25-26*). If we wait, we will later 'own his way: How wise, how strong his hand' (v.9.3, 4).

The essence of the message of the hymn could be said to be in v.10. We cannot understand God; we *can* trust him: "For my thoughts are not your thoughts, neither are your ways my ways, saith the Lord. For as the heavens are higher than the earth, so are my ways higher than your ways, and my thoughts than your thoughts" (*Isaiah 55:8, 9*). Thus in v.11 we pray to God for strength, for he knows our weakness. The phrases of the prayer are also from Isaiah: "Strengthen ye the weak hands and confirm the feeble knees" (*Isaiah 35:3*).

The hymn concludes (v.12) by expressing our desire to declare God's steadfast truth, his love and his care for us. We trust in him in times of joy and in times of grief, and we long for others to do so too.

ETERNAL BEAM OF LIGHT DIVINE

"The Lord is my light and my salvation: whom shall I fear?"
(*Psalm 27:1*)

---

1 Eternal Beam of light divine,
Fountain of unexhausted love,
In whom the Father's glories shine
Through earth beneath, and heaven above;

2 Jesu, the weary wanderer's rest,
Give me thy easy yoke to bear,
With steadfast patience arm my breast,
With spotless love, and lowly fear.

3 Thankful I take the cup from thee,
Prepared and mingled by thy skill,
Though bitter to the taste it be,
Powerful the wounded soul to heal.

4 Be thou, O Rock of ages, nigh!
So shall each murmuring thought be gone,
And grief, and fear, and care, shall fly,
As clouds before the mid-day sun.

5 Speak to my warring passions, "Peace!"
Say to my trembling heart, "Be still!"
Thy power my strength and fortress is,
For all things serve thy sovereign will.

6 O death! where is thy sting? Where now
Thy boasted victory, O grave?
Who shall contend with God? or who
Can hurt whom God delights to save?

This hymn was first published in "Hymns and Sacred Poems", 1739, under the heading "In affliction", and in the 1780 hymnbook it is in the section "For believers suffering". But the hymn is not limited to the subject of suffering, and one hymnbook ("Congregational Praise") places it in a section on "The Life of Discipleship: hope, joy and peace". Few hymnbooks now include this hymn, yet it has been much praised. The Scottish hymnologist Geoffrey Sampson called it "the greatest of all Wesley's hymns". More recently, Eric Routley (in "Hymns Today and Tomorrow", 1964) has written "It is the greatest piece of Christian hymnic writing on the subject of Christian suffering and hope that can be found anywhere". Yet it has been omitted from 'Hymns and Psalms' (1983) the new hymnbook for Methodists.

Verses 1, 2 and 5 are quoted in George Eliot's novel "Adam Bede": ". . . as she (Dinah Morris) held the long brush, and swept, singing to herself in a very low tone—like a sweet summer murmur that you have to listen for very closely—one of Charles Wesley's hymns, 'Eternal Beam of light divine'."

Each verse of this hymn is a meditation on a verse of Scripture. It opens with praise to Jesus (vv.1,2); by fixing our attention on him, we gain confidence to pray (vv.2-5) and finally to praise him despite our suffering (v.6).

Verse 1 concentrates on Christ as God. He is "the brightness of his (God's) glory, and the express image of his person" (*Hebrews 1:3*). Wesley's phrase 'beam' (1.1) is a better translation than "brightness" for the original Greek. It is also an echo of the opening of Milton's "Paradise Lost" Book III, "Hail, Holy Light! offspring of heav'n firstborn,/Or of the Eternal co-eternal beam . . .". Christ is love (v.1.2) and he is the revelation of God to man (v.1.3, 4): "the Word was made flesh, and dwelt among us (and we beheld his glory, the glory as of the only begotten of the Father,)" (*John 1:14*).

In v.2 we can identify with the manhood of Jesus. We respond to his call and his promise, "Come unto me, and I will give you rest (v.2.1). Take my yoke upon you (v.2.2), and learn of me; for I am meek and lowly in heart: (v.2.3, 4). . . my yoke is easy, and my burden is light." (*Matthew 11:28-30*). 'Armed' with Christ's patience (i.e. endurance), love and fear (i.e. reverence) (v.2.3, 4), we can 'take the bitter cup' of v.3. The phrase evokes Jesus' prayer in Gethsemane (*Matthew 26:42*). Our sufferings become insignificant in the face of Christ's suffering. Our comfort is that the cup is from God, and what wounds us now, heals later (v.3.3, 4: see *Hebrews 12:3-13*).

We repeat the prayer for God's presence in v.4. 'Rock of Ages' (v.4.1), a phrase also in Toplady's well-known hymn, comes from the Hebrew of *Isaiah 26:4*, which may be translated as "Trust ye in the Lord for ever: for the Lord Jehovah is the Rock of Ages" (see AV margin). God's presence dispels our 'murmuring' (v.4.2)—a characteristic of the Children of Israel, who often "murmured" against God and Moses (e.g. *Exodus 17:3-6*). As well as grumbles, grief, fear and care evaporate (v.4.3).

"Peace: be still' (v.5.1, 2) were the words with which Jesus quelled the storm on the Sea of Galilee (*Mark 4:39*). Wesley applies these words to our conflicts and fears. Christ showed his power over nature, and his all-powerfulness is our comfort: "I will love thee, O Lord, my strength. The Lord is my rock, and my fortress, and my deliverer" (v.5.3; *Psalm 18:1-2*). The last line stresses God's sovereignty, reflecting David's prayer and praise in *1 Chronicles 29:10-13*.

The prayer ends in v.5; the answer is expressed in the words of Paul, paraphrased in v.6: "O death, where is thy sting? O grave, where is thy victory?" (*1 Corinthians 15:55*). These questions are answered in *1 Corinthians 15:57*. The final lines ask the questions of *Isaiah 50:8-9,* which are triumphantly answered in *Romans 8:31-39*. The hymn ends with four questions, but they are not doubts: the confident answers are clear.

FATHER IN WHOM WE LIVE

"The grace of the Lord Jesus Christ, the love of God, and the communion of the Holy Ghost . . ."

(*2 Corinthians 13:14*)

---

1 Father, in whom we live,
In whom we are, and move,
The glory, power, and praise receive
Of thy creating love.
Let all the angel-throng
Give thanks to God on high;
While earth repeats the joyful song,
And echoes to the sky.

2 Incarnate Deity,
Let all the ransomed race
Render in thanks their lives to thee,
For thy redeeming grace.
The grace to sinners showed
Ye heavenly choirs proclaim,
And cry, "Salvation to our God,
Salvation to the Lamb!"

3 Spirit of Holiness,
Let all thy saints adore
Thy sacred energy, and bless
Thine heart-renewing power.
Not angel-tongues can tell
Thy love's ecstatic height,
The glorious joy unspeakable,
The beatific sight.

4 Eternal, Triune Lord!
Let all the hosts above,
Let all the sons of men, record
And dwell upon thy love.
When heaven and earth are fled
Before thy glorious face,
Sing all the saints thy love hath made
Thine everlasting praise!

This hymn was first published in 1747 in "Hymns for those that seek and those that have Redemption in the Blood of Jesus Christ" with the title "To The Trinity". It was not originally included in John Wesley's 1780 hymnbook, but was added after his death in the section entitled "For Believers Rejoicing".

A four-verse hymn which addresses in turn God the Father, God the Son, God the Holy Spirit, and God the Trinity, is a helpful and appropriate form of Christian worship. A number of hymns by various authors follow this pattern, for example; "Thou whose Almighty Word". This hymn of Charles Wesley deserves to be better known.

The hymn starts by quoting from Paul's speech at Athens (*Acts 17:28*), though this in itself is a quotation from the Greek poet Epimenides: "In him we live and move and have our being". Thus, the hymn is expressing a widely accepted belief in God. We praise him 'for his creating love' (v.1.4): "Thou art worthy O Lord to receive glory and honour and power: for thou hast created all things" (*Revelation 4:11*). Angels and men join in this praise (v.1.5-8), echoing the words of the Psalmist, "Praise ye him, all his angels: praise ye him, all his hosts" (*Psalm 148:2*).

Verse 2 moves from praise to God the Creator, to specifically Christian sentiments. We praise Jesus, the 'Incarnate Deity' (v.2.1) 'for his redeeming grace' (v.2.4). We offer our lives to him in thankfulness (v.2.3), and join the angels' song in Revelation (v.2.5-8; *Revelation 7:9, 10*).

Jesus' promise to the disciples as he departed at the Ascension was "Ye shall receive power, after that the Holy Ghost is come upon you" (*Acts 1:8*). Verse 3 praises God the Holy Spirit for his 'heart-renewing power' (v.3.4). Even angels cannot fully tell his gifts (v.3.5-8): only humankind experience his gifts of grace and love. Charles Wesley shares St. Paul's thrill at the heavenly glories revealed to man by the Holy Spirit: (*1 Corinthians 2:9, 10*). The Spirit's chief work is to reveal Christ and strengthen our faith in the one "whom having not seen, ye love: in whom, though now ye see him not, yet believing, ye rejoice with joy unspeakable (v.3.7) and full of glory (v.3.8)" (*1 Peter 1:8*).

The final verse praises God the Trinity: 'Triune' meaning "three in one". Once again, heaven and earth join in the praise. We 'dwell upon thy love' (v.4.4). 'Love' or 'Grace' has been praised in every verse of the hymn, and here we refer to both the present and the future. When "earth and heaven flee away" (v.4.5; *Revelation 20:11*) we can and will continue to praise God.

FATHER, WHOSE EVERLASTING LOVE THY ONLY SON FOR SINNERS GAVE

"For God so loved the world, that he gave his only begotten Son, that whosoever believeth in him should not perish, but have everlasting life. For God sent not his Son into the world to condemn the world; but that the world through him might be saved."

(*John 3:16-17*)

---

1 Father, whose everlasting love
Thy only Son for sinners gave,
Whose grace to all did freely move,
And sent him down the world to save;

2 Help us thy mercy to extol,
Immense, unfathomed, unconfined;
To praise the Lamb who died for all,
The general Saviour of mankind.

3 Thy undistinguishing regard
Was cast on Adam's fallen race;
For all thou hast in Christ prepared
Sufficient, sovereign, saving grace.

4 The world he suffered to redeem;
For all he hath the atonement made;
For those that will not come to him
The ransom of his life was paid.

5 Arise, O God, maintain thy cause!
The fulness of the Gentiles call;
Lift up the standard of thy cross,
And all shall own thou diedst for all.

This hymn was first published in "Hymns on God's Everlasting Love" in 1741. Originally it had no fewer than 17 verses. John Wesley omitted it from the first edition (1780) of "Wesley's Hymns", but later editions included six verses (originally nos. 1, 2, 3, 7, 12, 17). Five of the six verses chosen by Wesley remain unchanged in "The Methodist Hymn Book" and in a few other modern hymnbooks. This is one example of many excellent hymns by Charles Wesley which would enrich worship if only the hymn was more widely available.

At first sight, this is simply a hymn of praise for God's goodness—in "Wesley's Hymns" it was placed in the section entitled 'Describing the Goodness of God'. But the hymn had another role as well: it has been described as "the battle-song of militant Arminianism against a debased Calvinism". Arminius was a Dutch theologian who strongly opposed the Calvinists' view that salvation is available only to the 'elect'. In the early years of Methodism there was a major division between those who supported and those who opposed the Calvinist viewpoint. The doctrinal position of the brothers John and Charles Wesley can be best summarized as Evangelical as well as Arminian: not that all *will* be saved, but that all *can* be saved. In this hymn, the word 'ALL' appears in every verse: (v.1.3) "Whose grace to ALL did freely move"; (v.2.3) "To praise the Lamb who died for ALL"; (v.3.3) "For ALL thou hast in Christ prepared Sufficient, sovereign, saving grace"; (v.4.2) "For ALL He hath atonement made"; (v.5.4) "And ALL shall own he died for ALL". Other phrases emphasize these points, and also display very well Wesley's ability to weave long words into both the meaning and the metre of a verse: "Thy mercy . . . unconfined" (v.2.1, 2); "The general Saviour of mankind" (v.2.4); "Thy undistinguishing regard" (v.3.1).

Verses 1 and 2 are one sentence: the main verb does not appear until the fifth line; "Father . . . help us to extol Thy mercy . . . (and) to praise the Lamb who died for all". We ask for God's help in our praise because, unaided, our praise is totally inadequate by comparison with his "immense, unfathomed, unconfined mercy" (v.2.2). God's love and grace is both everlasting (v.1.1) and linked with a specific event in history (v.1.4).

Wesley emphasizes God's "undistinguishing regard" for mankind (v.3.1). Not only did this have the doctrinal implications explained above, but the church of the eighteenth century ignored the poor and forgot the new industrial areas: the message "for all" was—and still is—a radical one. The "sufficient, sovereign, saving grace" (v.3.4) is for all—but individuals still have to respond individually. Wesley is following closely the teaching of the Apostle Paul: "My grace is sufficient for thee" (*2 Corinthians 12:9*) was God's message to Paul. ". . . the righteousness of God, which is by faith of Jesus Christ unto *all*, and upon *all* them that believe" (*Romans 3:22*) was Paul's message to Christians in Rome.

The vision of the whole world is prominent throughout the hymn, and particularly in v.4: "*the world* he suffered to redeem" (v.4.1). Wesley was the first hymn-writer to have worked in the New World as well as in the Old World, and this new awareness of the world's needs is clearly evident. Thus the final verse appropriately concludes with a prayer for God's kingdom to spread. The Wesley brothers did more than almost anyone else to spread the kingdom, yet they recognized that the power is God's, not their own. "The fulness of the Gentiles" (v.5.2) is another of Paul's phrases (*Romans 11:25*): Wesley follows the example of the Apostle Paul in seeking the salvation of the whole world.

FORTH IN THY NAME, O LORD, I GO

"I have set the Lord always before me"
(*Psalm 16:8*)

1 Forth in thy name, O Lord, I go,
My daily labour to pursue,
Thee, only thee, resolved to know,
In all I think, or speak, or do.

2 The task thy wisdom has assigned,
O let me cheerfully fulfil,
In all my works thy presence find,
And prove thy acceptable will!

3 Thee may I set at my right hand,
Whose eyes my inmost substance see;
And labour on at thy command,
And offer all my works to thee.

4 Give me to bear thy easy yoke,
And every moment watch and pray,
And still to things eternal look,
And hasten to thy glorious day.

5 For thee delightfully employ
Whate'er thy bounteous grace hath given;
And run my course with even joy,
And closely walk with thee to heaven.

There are few hymns about our working hours. This is extraordinary, since work occupies such a large and important part of our lives, and most people are familiar with the idea of singing a hymn at school before starting the day's work. The well-known hymns about work can be counted on the fingers of one hand.

"Wesley's Hymns" had a specific section entitled "For Believers Working", with eight hymns—appropriate in a hymnbook called "a little body of experimental and *practical* divinity". Wesley preached Christianity as a religion for the real world. One hymn in this section is entitled "Son of a Carpenter" and begins with the fine couplet:

Servant of all, to toil for men
Thou didst not, Lord, refuse.

Another of the hymns suggests purpose and meaning in work:

End of my every action thou,
In all things thee I see:
Accept my hallowed labour now,
I do it unto thee.

The finest hymn on work, however, is unquestionably the one printed here. It was first published in 1749 in "Hymns and Sacred Poems" with the title "For believers before work". Verse 3 of the original was omitted from the 1780 hymnbook, and has been omitted from most books since; nevertheless it has some helpful phrases, even if it is unsuitable for public worship:-

Preserve me from my calling's snare,
And hide my simple heart above,
Above the thorns of choking care,
The gilded baits of worldly love.

"Go forth into the world in peace . . ." is a familiar exhortation to many Christians. Charles Wesley applies this idea specifically to our daily work (v.1.1, 2), following *Psalm 104:23*: "Man goeth forth unto his work and to his labour until the evening". All we think, speak, or do (v.1.4) is to be in tune with our faith: "whatsoever ye do, in word or deed, do all in the name of the Lord Jesus" (*Colossians 3:17*).

Wesley recognizes (v.2.1) that we are 'assigned' to our task—and that this assignment is an aspect of God's wisdom. We pray for cheerfulness at work (v.2.2); we pray also that we may find God's presence through our work (v.2.3). 'Thy acceptable will' (v.2.4) is from *Romans 12:2*: "Be not conformed to this world: but be ye transformed by the renewing of your mind, that ye may prove what is that good, and acceptable, and perfect, will of God". 'Acceptable' is accented differently now from Wesley's day, so to keep the metre this is usually changed to 'thy good and perfect will'—words from the same Bible verse.

The idea of offering our work to God (v.3.4) is a very ancient one. The "firstfruits" of the harvest were offered to God in Old Testament times, and harvest festivals are still popular. The offering of all our work is a more important and profound truth. It is, perhaps, less popular, but it is at the heart of a faith which calls us to "offer ourselves as a living sacrifice" (*Romans 12:1*): this offering must include all our work. Even so, this can still be called 'an easy yoke': we offer ourselves to the Christ who said "Come unto me all ye that labour . . . Take my yoke upon you and learn of me . . . For my yoke is easy, and my burden is light" (*Matthew 11: 28-30*). Our work and our looking forward are two sides of the same coin: our work is important, but not the sole purpose of life (v.4.3, 4). So we are to use our gifts in our work—gifts which are given by God's 'bounteous grace' (v.5.2), and we are to walk closely with God (v.5.4) at the same time.

JESU, LOVER OF MY SOUL

"A man shall be as an hiding place from the wind, and a covert from the tempest" (*Isaiah 32:2*)

1 Jesu, Lover of my soul,
Let me to Thy bosom fly,
While the nearer waters roll,
While the tempest still is high:
Hide me, O my Saviour, hide,
Till the storm of life be past;
Safe into the haven guide,
Oh receive my soul at last.

2 Other refuge have I none;
Hangs my helpless soul on Thee;
Leave, ah! leave me not alone,
Still support and comfort me:
All my trust on Thee is stayed,
All my help from Thee I bring;
Cover my defenceless head
With the shadow of Thy wing.

3 Thou, O Christ, art all I want;
More than all in Thee I find,
Raise the fallen, cheer the faint,
Heal the sick, and lead the blind:
Just and holy is Thy name,
I am all unrighteousness;
False and full of sin I am,
Thou art full of truth and grace.

4 Plenteous grace with Thee is found,
Grace to cover all my sin;
Let the healing streams abound,
Make and keep me pure within:
Thou of life the fountain art,
Freely let me take of Thee,
Spring Thou up within my heart,
Rise to all eternity.

This hymn was first published in 1740 in "Hymns and Sacred Poems". The title was "In Time of Danger and Temptation". It soon appeared in some Anglican hymnbooks, but was not included in the 1780 Wesleyan hymnbook, as John Wesley thought the opening line too familiar. However, it was added to "Wesley's Hymns" shortly after his death.

Numerous alterations have been attempted to v.1, but few have survived, and Charles Wesley's original version is normally used now. "The nearer waters roll" in v.1.3 is a phrase from Matthew Prior's poem "Solomon, and the vanity of knowledge". Prior was a poet much admired by the Wesleys and their contemporaries. Originally, the hymn had five verses, but the original v.3 is almost always omitted now:-

Wilt thou not regard my call?
Wilt thou not accept my prayer?
Lo! I sink, I faint, I fall—
Lo! On thee I cast my care!
Reach me out thy gracious hand:
While I of thy strength receive,
Hoping against hope I stand,
Dying, and behold I live!

Several stories exist about the origin of this hymn, but they are unsubstantiated.

The biblical origin of the first line of this hymn has often passed unrecognized. The Book of Wisdom, in the Apocrypha, includes the verse, "Thou sparest all; for they are thine, O Lord, thou lover of souls" (*Wisdom 11:26*). Also, King Hezekiah said, "Thou hast in love to my soul delivered it from the pit of corruption" (*Isaiah 38:17*).

The metaphors of the hymn are a helpful means of thinking about danger and temptation. Criticism has been voiced at the mixing of metaphors, but this is to misunderstand their purpose: none is a full picture, but all offer helpful insights. The prayer to 'hide' in Christ (v.1.5) is to give us strength to face dangers and temptations, not to retreat permanently from involvement with the world. Wesley's hymns about work (see p.42) indicate clearly that he did not preach a quietist, 'other-worldly' religion. Indeed, he wrote many hymns to oppose the teaching of the Quietists (see p.10).

The description of the storm in v.1 is partly based on Psalm 107: 23-30, which vividly describe a storm, after which "he bringeth them unto their desired haven" (*Psalm 107:30;* v.1.7). Doubtless *Isaiah 32:2* (opposite) was also in Charles Wesley's mind.

"God is our refuge and strength, a very present help in trouble" (*Psalm 46:1*) is the theme of v.2. God as our only safe refuge is a constant theme in the Bible. The verse, "Hide me under the shadow of thy wings" (*Psalm 17:8*), is the source of the last line.

Verse 3 speaks of the all-sufficiency of Christ to meet every human need, for "Christ is all, and in all" (*Colossians 3:11*). Christ's miracles are alluded to in lines 3.4: he is still the divine healer, bringing both spiritual and physical well-being. The latter part of v.3 is exceptionally fine poetry—it has been called "the finest double chiasmus in the English language". The rhymes are in an A B A B sequence, but the themes within the four lines follow an A B B A sequence. In addition to this literary excellence, Wesley manages to quote the Bible: Jesus is "full of grace and truth" (v.2.8 *John 1:14*).

The last word in v.3 is Grace, and this word in v.4 resolves the conflict of our sinfulness and Christ's holiness. We pray for Christ the Redeemer to make and to keep us pure (v.4.4). The glorified Christ promises "I will give unto him that is athirst of the fountain of the water of life freely" (*Revelation 21:6*). In nature, a fountain and a spring lead on to streams and flowing water: the imagery of water in this verse conveys the idea of the source of the new life (v.4.5), of healing power (v.4.3) and of constant refreshment (v.4.6) throughout this life and the next.

JESUS, THE NAME HIGH OVER ALL

"God also hath . . . given him a name which is above every name: That at the name of Jesus every knee should bow . . ."
(*Philippians 2:9-10*)

---

1 Jesus! the name high over all,
In hell, or earth, or sky,
Angels and men before it fall,
And devils fear and fly.

2 Jesus! the name to sinners dear,
The name to sinners given;
It scatters all their guilty fear,
It turns their hell to heaven.

3 Jesus! the prisoner's fetters breaks,
And bruises Satan's head;
Power into strengthless souls it speaks,
And life into the dead.

4 O that the world might taste and see
The riches of his grace!
The arms of love that compass me
Would all mankind embrace.

5 His only righteousness I show,
His saving truth proclaim,
'Tis all my business here below,
To cry, "Behold the Lamb!"

6 Happy, if with my latest breath
I may but gasp his name;
Preach him to all, and cry in death,
"Behold, behold the Lamb!"

Originally, this hymn had 22 verses! It was first published in "Hymns and Sacred Poems" in 1749, with the title "Jesus, all in all" and was to be sung "After preaching in a Church". By 1780, John Wesley had reduced it to six verses, and placed it in the section "The Goodness of God". In this form it is found, usually unchanged, in many hymnbooks today. The verses selected are 9, 10, 12, 13, 18 and 22. The original first verse began "Jesus, accept the grateful songs".

Two aspects of the hymn typify Charles Wesley's theology: first, his emphasis on the name of Jesus—knowing that in the Bible a *name* reflects the *nature* and character of a person (see also p.16). Second, the stress is on the universality of Christ's love and salvation—seen especially in v.4.

Verse 1 speaks of Jesus in majesty, as described by Paul in *Philippians 2:9-10.* This is a much-quoted passage, and the inspiration for many other hymns as well, e.g. "At the name of Jesus, every knee shall bow". Verse 2 is in marked contrast—a contrast that is at the heart of the Christian faith. Jesus' name is indeed above every name, but the name "Jesus" means "Saviour" (*Matthew 1:21*) and thus 'our hell' can turn to heaven (v.2.4).

After reflecting on Jesus in majesty and Jesus the Saviour, Jesus the all-powerful is the theme of v.3: "The Lord looseth the prisoners" (*Psalm 146:7*) starts the verse. His conquest of Satan (v.3.2) is expressed in the words of *Genesis 3:15*—a passage we hear as a prophecy of the Messiah at many Festivals of Nine Lessons and Carols at Christmas. The latter part of v.3 speaks of his power becoming ours: through him (v.3.3) we can become "strong in the Lord and in the power of his might" (*Ephesians 6:10*). And our death can become life: "in Christ shall all be made alive" (v.3.4; *1 Corinthians 15:22*).

The Christian faith is not a selfish religion. Verse 4 prays for the message to reach outwards to the whole world. All must be invited: "O taste and see that the Lord is good" (v.4.1; *Psalm 34:8*). 'The riches of his grace' (v.4.2; *Ephesians 1:7*) are available to all (v.4. 3, 4).

Verses 5 and 6 link the themes of Jesus' majesty, saving grace and power (vv.1 to 3) with the evangelism envisaged in v.4. The scriptural basis of these verses includes *1 Corinthians 1:30,* "Christ Jesus, who of God is made unto us wisdom, and righteousness (v.5.1) and sanctification and redemption" (v.5.2). We are happy if we 'preach him to all' (v.6. 1-3), for "Woe is unto me if I preach not the Gospel" (*1 Corinthians 9:16*). The hymn concludes with the words of John the Baptist: "Behold the Lamb of God, which taketh away the sin of the world" (*John 1:29*).

JESU, THY BLOOD AND RIGHTEOUSNESS

"Christ Jesus, who of God is made unto us . . . righteousness"
(*1 Corinthians 1:30*)

1 Jesu, thy blood and righteousness
My beauty are, my glorious dress;
Midst flaming worlds in these arrayed,
With joy shall I lift up my head.

2 Bold shall I stand in thy great day,
For who aught to my charge shall lay?
Fully absolved through these I am,
From sin and fear, from guilt and
shame.

3 The holy, meek, unspotted Lamb,
Who from the Father's bosom came,
Who died for me, even me, to atone,
Now for my Lord and God I own.

4 Lord, I believe thy precious blood,
Which at the mercy-seat of God
For ever doth for sinners plead,
For me, even for my soul, was shed.

5 Lord, I believe, were sinners more
Than sands upon the ocean shore,
Thou hast for all a ransom paid,
For all a full atonement made.

6 When from the dust of death I rise,
To claim my mansion in the skies,
Even then this shall be all my plea,
Jesus hath lived, hath died, for me.

7 Thus Abraham, the friend of God,
Thus all heaven's armies bought with
blood,
Saviour of sinners thee proclaim;
Sinners, of whom the chief I am.

8 Jesu, be endless praise to thee,
Whose boundless mercy hath for me,
For me and all thy hands have made,
An everlasting ransom paid.

9 Ah! give to all thy servants, Lord,
With power to speak thy gracious word,
That all who to thy wounds will flee,
May find eternal life in thee.

10 Thou God of power, thou God of love,
Let the whole world thy mercy prove!
Now let thy words o'er all prevail;
Now take the spoils of death and hell.

11 O let the dead now hear thy voice,
Now bid thy banished ones rejoice,
Their beauty this, their glorious dress,
Jesu, thy blood and righteousness!

This is another of the 33 hymns translated from German by John Wesley. It was written by Nicolaus Ludwig, Count von Zinzendorf (1700-1760)—a remarkable Lutheran landowner whom John Wesley met when in Germany soon after his conversion in 1738. Zinzendorf was son of the Prime Minister of Saxony, born in Dresden, and educated in Halle and Wittenberg. He created the settlement of Herrenhut on his estates for Moravians, who were Protestant refugees from what is now part of Czechoslovakia. They formed a close-knit community, and in 1737 Zinzendorf became their Bishop. He encouraged missionary work, and travelled in England and America promoting his ideas for Christian communities.

During his life, the Count wrote over 2,000 hymns. This one was written in 1739 on St. Eustatius, a small West Indian island that still belongs to the Netherlands. Published the same year in the "Herrenhut Gesang Buch", it had 33 verses originally. In his translation, John Wesley omitted nine, and published the rest in "Hymns and Sacred Poems" in 1740. In his 1780 hymnbook there were 11 verses; this is the version printed here.

Jesus' blood and righteousness (v.1.1 and v.11.4) are the basis of our faith. It is through the death of the righteous Christ that humans can be accepted as righteous by God. The hymn takes up biblical allusions to righteousness being a garment, which is a gift of God and inherently beautiful like a bridal robe (v.1.2). Isaiah had prophesied, "I will greatly rejoice in the Lord . . . he hath covered me with the robe of righteousness . . ." (*Isaiah 61:10*). Paul relates the theme to the crucifixion and resurrection in *Romans 3:21-26*: "The righteousness of God" is now available "by faith of Jesus Christ" and is "upon all them that believe" (*Romans 3:22*). Thus dressed in the robe of righteousness, whatever happens we can 'lift up our heads with joy' (v.1.4), at the end of the world (v.1.3; *2 Peter 3:10-13*); on the day of judgment (v.2; *Romans 8:33-34*) and in eternal glory (*Revelation 7:9-15*). It is through Christ's blood and righteousness ('these', v.2.3) that we are freed 'from sin and fear, from guilt and shame' (v.2.4).

The hymn is in the singular throughout, for faith is personal. In v.3, 'I own' "the Lamb without blemish" (v.3.1; *1 Peter 1:18-19*), the Son of God (v.3.2; *John 1:18*) as 'my Lord and God' (v.3.4; *John 20:26-29*). The following two verses open with 'I believe . . .'—the first words of the Apostles' Creed. 'I believe' (v.4) that "by his own blood he entered once into the holy place, having obtained eternal redemption for us" (*Hebrews 9:12*). Furthermore, 'I believe' (v.5) that "Christ Jesus gave himself a ransom for all" (*1 Timothy 2:6*). This theme of Christ as universal Saviour was very important to the Wesleys (see p.47). Verse 6 might seem arrogant: 'to claim my mansion' indeed! But this *is* Christ's promise: 'In my father's house are many mansions . . . I go to prepare a place for you" (*John 14:2*). Our only 'plea' is Jesus' life, and his death (v.6.3, 4).

Verse 7 stresses again the centrality of faith: "Abraham believed God, and it was imputed unto him for righteousness: and he was called the Friend of God" (v.7.1; *James 2:23*; also *Romans 4:3, 9; Galatians 3:6*). So all in heaven (v.7.2) praise God that Jesus has "redeemed us to God by thy blood" (*Revelation 5:9*). And we are invited to identify with the author, the translator and the Apostle Paul and acknowledge "that Christ Jesus came into the world to save sinners, of whom I am the chief" (v.7.4; *1 Timothy 1:15*).

This leads to a fine verse of praise for personal salvation which is everlasting (v.8.4) and available to all (v.8.3). And so we pray (v.9) for *power* to preach the Lord's word that all may find salvation. We pray to the 'God of power' (v.10.1), so often called "the Lord God Almighty" in the Bible, who also reveals himself as the God of love (v.10.1; *1 John 4:16*). In the early church, "mightily grew the word of God and prevailed" (*Acts 19:20*), and we pray for the same to be true today (v.10.3). Christ is victorious, and the 'spoils of death and hell' belong to him (v.10.4; *Revelation 1:18*). Thus we anticipate Christ's final victory in the final verse. A prayer is made of Christ's words, "The dead shall hear the voice of the Son of God; and they that hear shall live" (v.11.1; *John 5:25*). Appropriately, the final line returns to the opening line of the hymn, for his victory is ours through his blood and righteousness.

JESUS, WE THUS OBEY

"This do in remembrance of me" (*Luke 22:19*)

1 Jesus, we thus obey
Thy last and kindest word;
Here, in Thine own appointed way,
We come to meet Thee, Lord.

2 Our hearts we open wide,
To make the Saviour room;
And lo! the Lamb, the Crucified,
The sinner's Friend, is come.

3 Thus we remember Thee,
And take this bread and wine
As Thine own dying legacy,
And our redemption's sign.

4 Thy presence makes the feast;
Now let our spirits feel
The glory not to be expressed,
The joy unspeakable.

5 With high and heavenly bliss
Thou dost our spirits cheer;
Thy house of banqueting is this,
And Thou hast brought us here.

6 Now let our souls be fed
With manna from above,
And over us Thy banner spread
Of everlasting love.

This is part of a longer hymn which was first published in "Hymns on the Lord's Supper" in 1745. Charles Wesley published many hymns on the Lord's Supper, both in his 1745 book and in other volumes. He saw the service as a central feature of Christian worship. Yet none of these appeared in "Wesley's Hymns" until 19th century supplements added hymns for special services. Both John and Charles Wesley maintained their membership of the Anglican church, and regarded their "Societies of people called Methodists" as part of the Church of England. In the early days, separate communion services were only held when the local Anglican church excluded Society members, or held communion services too infrequently for the Methodists.

Sadly, the Lord's Supper still divides Christians, but some of Wesley's hymns on the Lord's Supper are sung in almost all branches of the Christian church: an impressive testimony to the amount of agreement on the meaning of the service.

We obey (v.1.1) our Lord's words "Do this, in remembrance of me" (*Luke 22:19*), at every Lord's Supper. 'Thy last and kindest words' (v.1.2) were among the last words to the disciples before the crucifixion, and speak of the shed blood of the Saviour. "Greater love hath no man than this, that a man lay down his life for his friends" (*John 15:13*) said Jesus at that Last Supper with his disciples. We come to meet Christ (v.1.4) because we have his promise that "where two or three are gathered together in my name, there am I in the midst of them" (*Matthew 18:20*); Wesley himself believed that the communion service was an important means of grace.

There was "no room in the inn" when Jesus was born; in contrast, in v.2 we 'make room' for the Saviour in our hearts. Jesus is present as 'Lamb of God' (v.2.3) and 'friend of sinners' (v.2.4). The bread and wine are the 'sign of our redemption' (v.3.2-4) and Christ's presence 'makes the feast' (v.4.1). Here, as in many of his communion hymns, Wesley links together Calvary and heaven itself: at the Lord's Supper we remember the Lord's death (vv.2, 3) and anticipate the future marriage supper of the Lamb (vv.4, 5). In the present, Christ lives in the hearts of individuals and among the congregation, bringing joy. The words of v.4 are based on *1 Peter 1:8-9*: "Though now ye see him not, yet, believing, ye rejoice with joy unspeakable and full of glory" (v.3, 4).

"God hath blessed us with all spiritual blessings in heavenly places in Christ" (*Ephesians 1:3*) is the source of v.5. Although the Lord's Supper originated on a solemn occasion, the celebration is now a joyful time, and can even be called a 'banquet' (v.5.3). Wesley had in mind an Old Testament verse, "He brought me to the banqueting house, and his banner over me was love" (*Song of Solomon 2:4*), for another phrase from this verse concludes the hymn (v.6.3, 4). The 'manna from above' is Jesus himself, as he promised when elaborating on his claim "I am the bread of life" (see *John 6:48-58*).

LOVE DIVINE, ALL LOVES EXCELLING

"O visit me with thy salvation" (*Psalm 106:4*)

---

1 Love Divine, all loves excelling,
Joy of heaven, to earth come down;
Fix in us Thy humble dwelling,
All Thy faithful mercies crown.
Jesus, Thou art all compassion;
Pure, unbounded love Thou art;
Visit us with Thy salvation,
Enter every longing heart.

2 Breathe, oh breathe Thy loving Spirit
Into every troubled breast;
Let us all in Thee inherit,
Let us find Thy promised rest;
Take away the love of sinning,
Alpha and Omega be;
End of faith, as its beginning,
Set our hearts at liberty.

3 Come, almighty to deliver,
Let us all Thy life receive;
Suddenly return, and never,
Never more Thy temples leave.
Thee we would be always blessing,
Serve Thee as Thy hosts above;
Pray, and praise Thee without ceasing,
Glory in Thy perfect love.

4 Finish, then, Thy new creation;
Pure and spotless may we be;
Let us see Thy great salvation,
Perfectly restored in Thee;
Changed from glory into glory,
Till in heaven we take our place;
Till we cast our crowns before Thee,
Lost in wonder, love, and praise.

This hymn was first published in 1747, in "Hymns for those that seek, and those that have Redemption in the Blood of Jesus Christ". In the 1780 hymnbook, verse 2 was omitted, but it had already appeared in other hymnbooks, and can still be found today in some books (e.g. 'Christian Worship'), hence it is included here.

The metre and the first line of the hymn are based on Dryden's "King Arthur":

Fairest Isle, all Isles excelling
Seat of pleasures and of loves
Venus here will choose her dwelling
And forsake her Cyprian groves.

The last line of the hymn is taken from another poet, but this time the context is a Christian hymn: it is the last line of Addison's, "When all thy mercies, O my God". There have been several minor amendments to the words, some by John Wesley. For example, v.2.4 originally read "that second rest", and v.2.5, "our power of sinning"; the revised wording is closer to Scripture.

"Love Divine" (v.1.1) and "Joy of Heaven" (v.1.2) are titles of Christ, so this hymn is a prayer to Christ. We pray 'Fix in us thy humble dwelling': a puzzling phrase until it is linked with the verse "the tabernacle of God is with men, and he will dwell with them" (*Revelation 21:3*). The "tabernacle" was originally a humble tent. Because of the compassion and love of Jesus (v.1.5-6), we can ask him into our hearts (v.1.8). 'Visit' (v.1.7) is a strong verb: this is an invitation to Jesus to come *and to stay* (*John 14:23*).

Verse 2, often omitted, continues the prayer to Christ. This time, we ask him to 'breathe' his Spirit into us, as he did to his disciples after his resurrection (*John 20:22*). We also ask for his 'promised rest' (v.2.4), for Jesus said, "Come unto me, all ye that labour and are heavy laden, and I will give you rest" (*Matthew 11:28-29*). We ask him to be our 'Alpha and Omega': the theme and biblical references are similar to those in Wesley's hymn "Jesus the first and last" (p.64). The reference to our 'love of sinning' (v.2.5), and the prayer for liberty (v.2.8), make clear the meaning of the prayer for deliverance (v.3.1): this is deliverance from sin, into the "glorious liberty of the children of God" (*Romans 8:21*). Without v.2, the sense of v.3 is less clear.

In this third verse, we ask to receive Christ's life (v.3.2): 'life' was Charles Wesley's original wording, although John altered it to 'grace' in his 1780 hymnbook, and many other books follow this alteration. Wesley often talked about souls filled with the "life of God", and the ideas of new life in Christ and being "born again" to eternal life are central to the Gospel. Such life is the free gift of God's grace. In asking for life, we are asking for Christ himself (v.3.3). In this case, the author's inspiration is the prophet Malachi, "The Lord whom ye seek shall suddenly come to his temple" (*Malachi 3:1*). This is reinterpreted in the light of St. Paul's reminder to the Christians in Corinth that they are 'the temple of the living God' (*2 Corinthians 6:16;* see also *1 Corinthians 3:16*). These lines, therefore, are a direct prayer for Christ's continual presence in each one of us (v.3.3-4). Thus we seek to pray, praise and serve God (v.3.6-7): "Blessed are they that dwell in thy house: they will be still praising thee" (*Psalm 84:4*).

The final verse looks forward. Once again the imagery is biblical. "We are changed into the same image (as Christ), from glory to glory" (v.4.5; *2 Corinthians 3:18*). Wesley applies to all Christians a verse from Revelation (v.4.7): "The elders fall down before him . . . and worship him . . . and cast their crowns before the throne, saying, Thou art worthy, O Lord, to receive glory and honour and power: for thou hast created all things, and for thy pleasure they are and were created." (*Revelation 4:10-11*). Thus we become 'lost in wonder, love, and praise' (v.4.8).

O FOR A HEART TO PRAISE MY GOD

"Make me a clean heart, O God"
(*Psalm 51:10*) (Prayer Book version)

---

1 O for a heart to praise my God,
A heart from sin set free!
A heart that always feels thy blood
So freely spilt for me!

2 A heart resigned, submissive, meek,
My great Redeemer's throne,
Where only Christ is heard to speak,
Where Jesus reigns alone;

3 An humble, lowly, contrite heart
Believing, true, and clean;
Which neither life nor death can part
From him that dwells within;

4 A heart in every thought renewed,
And full of love divine;
Perfect, and right, and pure, and good,
A copy, Lord of thine!

5 Thy nature, gracious Lord, impart!
Come quickly from above,
Write thy new name upon my heart,
Thy new, best name of love.

The above verse from Psalm 51 was Wesley's own title for this hymn. It was first published in 1742 in "Hymns and Sacred Poems", under the heading "Holiness Desired". In the 1780 hymnbook, it comes in the section "For believers seeking for full redemption". Originally, the hymn had eight verses, but vv.5, 6 and 7 are normally now omitted.

This hymn is a simple yet profound prayer for God's presence. Theologians have argued over the Wesleys' view of "Christian perfection", and the two brothers were not always fully agreed on whether perfection can be achieved in this life. This hymn has sometimes been used as evidence for one viewpoint or another. In fact, it is a simple prayer for God's presence in us, echoing the sentiments of the penitential Psalm 51, and the Prayer Book phrases so familiar to the Wesleys: ". . . that we may hereafter live a godly, righteous, and sober life" and ". . . let us beseech Him to grant us true repentance, and His Holy Spirit . . . that the rest of our life hereafter may be pure and holy".

Verse 1 echoes David's penitence: "Hide thy face from my sins, and blot out all mine iniquities; create in me a clean heart O God" (*Psalm 51:9-10*). Several hymnbooks have used biblical phrases from *Hebrews 10:22* and *Matthew 26:28*, as an alternative conclusion to v.1:

A heart that's sprinkled with the blood
So freely shed for me.

Verses 2, 3 and 4 may seem at first sight to offer a negative and dull view of life: the adjectives at the start of each verse are not popular ones today. But these words cease to be negative as soon as 'my Great Redeemer's throne' (v.2.2) is reflected on. This is a remarkable claim made by Christians, and is the essence of the hymn. "Know ye not that ye are the temple of God, and that the Spirit of God dwelleth in you?" (*1 Corinthians 3:16*).

Verse 3 opens with another reference to *Psalm 51*: "The sacrifices of God are a broken spirit: a broken and a contrite heart O God thou wilt not despise" (*Psalm 51:17*). And this verse ends with a restatement of Paul's words, "Neither death nor life . . . shall be able to separate us from the love of God, which is in Christ Jesus our Lord" (*Romans 8:38-39*). Verse 4 also uses Paul's words, and every line can be traced to a verse from one of his epistles: v.4.1—". . . be ye transformed by the renewing of your mind" (*Romans 12:2*); v.4.2—". . . the love of God is shed abroad in our hearts by the Holy Ghost which is given unto us" (*Romans 5:5*); "And this I pray, that your love may abound yet more and more . . .; v.4.3— . . . that ye may be sincere and without offence till the day of Christ; being filled with the fruits of righteousness, which are by Jesus Christ, unto the glory and praise of God" (*Philippians 1:9-11*); v.4.4—"Let this mind be in you, which was also in Christ Jesus" (*Philippians 2:5*).

The last verse thus sums up the prayer: we seek to be transformed into Christ's image. "I will write upon him my new name" is a promise in *Revelation 3:12*. The 'new name' (v.5.3) is God's very nature—Love. The prayer continues to the end of the hymn: there is no easy solution offered to the quest for holiness. The hymn may seem introspective in parts, but it looks upward to Jesus as well as inwards. The author is, of course, also the author of "Soldiers of Christ arise" (p.58), and the contrasting concepts of both hymns are needed for a true understanding of the Christian faith.

O THOU WHO CAMEST FROM ABOVE

"The fire shall ever be burning upon the altar: it shall never be put out." (*Leviticus 6:13*)

---

1 O Thou who camest from above,
The pure celestial fire to impart,
Kindle a flame of sacred love
On the mean altar of my heart.

2 There let it for thy glory burn
With inextinguishable blaze,
And trembling to its source return
In humble prayer, and fervent praise.

3 Jesus, confirm my heart's desire
To work, and speak, and think for thee;
Still let me guard the holy fire,
And still stir up thy gift in me.

4 Ready for all thy perfect will,
My acts of faith and love repeat,
Till death thy endless mercies seal,
And make my sacrifice complete.

Some of Charles Wesley's finest hymns take one theme that is expounded throughout the hymn—for example *light* ("Christ whose glory fills the skies"), *armour* ("Soldiers of Christ arise"), and, as here, *fire*.

This hymn was published in 1762 in "Short Hymns on Select Passages of Scriture"—a two-volume work containing 2,030 hymns, ranging over the whole Bible. Often, Wesley's interpretation of a passage owes much to Matthew Henry's great Bible Commentary, which was first published in 1700. While based on Scripture, this hymn also expresses his own experience: Charles Wesley is reported to have said to Samuel Bradburn that his experience might almost at any time be found in the first two verses.

This hymn is firmly based on a passage in Leviticus that was well-known to the Wesleys, but much less familiar to most people today. Yet, in one respect at least, the words have acquired a greater relevance to today's world than when they were first written: the "inextinguishable blaze" (v.2.2) contrasts with the "fire extinguishers" we now find in any public building. At least one hymn book ("Songs of Praise") omitted the verse "because 'inextinguishable' cannot be properly sung"—editors thus destroyed the original sense of the hymn, and deprived congregations of this vivid, everyday metaphor.

The idea that fire is a precious commodity is difficult to conceive, until one remembers that matches are a relatively recent invention, and firemaking is a difficult art. But this is not a normal fire: it is "the pure celestial fire" (v.1.2), sent by God (*Leviticus 9:24*) and entrusted to the priests of the Tabernacle. Wesley's verse for this hymn is *Leviticus 6:13* (quoted opposite)—the fire must not go out because it indicated both God's presence and his acceptance of the people's sacrifice of animals for sin. The altar was for offering sacrifices to God; Wesley takes alongside this a New Testament idea ". . . present your bodies a living sacrifice, holy, acceptable unto God . . ." (*Romans 12:1*). Thus our heart becomes the altar (v.1.4) where the flame must never go out (v.2.2)—this time, the flame is God's love (v.1.3). As the incense burnt at the time of sacrifice ascended to God, the source of all our offerings, so our offering of 'humble prayer and fervent praise' must return to its source: God (v.2.3, 4).

Verse 3 is a prayer directly addressed to Jesus. In Leviticus, guarding the fire is the work of the priests. Now, we are "a royal priesthood" (*1 Peter 2:9*) and must guard the holy fire of God's love in our hearts (v.3.3) and do his perfect will (v.4.1; *Romans 12:2*). Wesley turns to the Greek of *2 Timothy 1:6*, where a word familiar to anyone lighting a fire is used by Paul: "I remind you to rekindle the gift of God that is within you . . ." (RSV), thus cleverly linking Old and New Testament. Our encouragement is that "it is God which worketh in you both to will and to do of his good pleasure" (*Philippians 2:13*); he will rekindle the gifts he gives (v.3.4) and the faith and love we show (v.4.2). Our sacrifice of prayer and praise on earth will be completed when we worship God face to face in heaven (v.4.3, 4).

SOLDIERS OF CHRIST ARISE

". . . be strong in the Lord, and in the power of his might. Put on the whole armour of God . . ." (*Ephesians 6:10-11*)

---

1 Soldiers of Christ, arise,
And put your armour on,
Strong in the strength which God supplies
Through his eternal Son;
Strong in the Lord of hosts,
And in his mighty power,
Who in the strength of Jesus trusts
Is more than conqueror.

2 Stand then in his great might,
With all his strength endued;
But take, to arm you for the fight,
The panoply of God;
That, having all things done,
And all your conflicts passed,
Ye may o'ercome through Christ alone,
And stand entire at last.

3 Leave no unguarded place,
No weakness of the soul,
Take every virtue, every grace,
And fortify the whole;
Indissolubly joined,
To battle all proceed;
But arm yourselves with all the mind
That was in Christ, your Head.

4 But, above all, lay hold
On faith's victorious shield;
Armed with that adamant and gold,
Be sure to win the field:
If faith surround your heart,
Satan shall be subdued,
Repelled his every fiery dart,
And quenched with Jesu's blood.

5 Jesus hath died for you!
What can his love withstand?
Believe, hold fast your shield, and who
Shall pluck you from his hand?
Believe that Jesus reigns,
All power to him is given;
Believe, till freed from sin's remains,
Believe yourselves to heaven!

6 To keep your armour bright,
Attend with constant care,
Still walking in your Captain's sight,
And watching unto prayer.
Ready for all alarms,
Steadfastly set your face,
And always exercise your arms,
And use your every grace.

7 Pray, without ceasing pray,
Your Captain gives the word;
His summons cheerfully obey,
And call upon the Lord;
To God your every want
In instant prayer display;
Pray always; pray, and never faint;
Pray, without ceasing pray!

8 In fellowship, alone,
To God with faith draw near,
Approach his courts, besiege his throne
With all the powers of prayer:
Go to his temple, go,
Nor from his altar move;
Let every house his worship know,
And every heart his love.

9 Pour out your souls to God,
And bow them with your knees,
And spread your hearts and hands abroad,
And pray for Zion's peace;
Your guides and brethren bear
For ever on your mind;
Extend the arms of mighty prayer,
In grasping all mankind.

10 From strength to strength go on,
Wrestle, and fight, and pray,
Tread all the powers of darkness down,
And win the well-fought day.
Still let the Spirit cry
In all His soldiers, "Come,"
Till Christ the Lord descend from high,
And take the conquerors home.

Wesley's hymn on *Ephesians 6:10-17* appeared as 16 verses, each of eight lines, in "Hymns and Sacred Poems", 1749. It was entitled "The Whole Armour of God". John Wesley's 1780 hymnbook included 12 verses, divided into three parts, under the heading "For believers fighting". Hymnbooks select various verses and parts of verses from the original. It is interesting to note how the selection colours the theme of the hymn: Part I and the final verse are about the soldier's conflict; other verses stress the armour, faith and prayer.

The picture of the Christian as a soldier armed for conflict is Paul's (*Ephesians 6:10-17*). The Apostle may well have had a Roman soldier in sight while he was writing (*Ephesians 6:20*).

The hymn emphasizes the context in which Paul wrote about "the whole armour of God", for the description of the armour ends with a colon (*Ephesians 6:17*) and the sentence continues "Praying always with all prayer and supplication in the Spirit . . ." (*Ephesians 6:18*).

The opening three verses follow closely *Ephesians 6:10-13*. Charles Wesley, the Greek scholar, goes back to the New Testament Greek for the correct word to fit the metre in v.2.4: the two English words "whole armour" (*Ephesians 6:11, 13*) translate the one Greek word, *panoplia* (panoply). His stress, like Paul's, is on God's spiritual strength and provision for fighting spiritual foes. But Wesley also manages to expand Paul's ideas by introducing the appropriate Old Testament title "Lord of Hosts" (v.1.5), and another Pauline reference, "We are more than conquerors through him that loved us" (*Romans 8:37*) at the end of v.1. "That . . . ye may o'ercome' (v.2.7) reflects the many promises made to "him that overcometh" by Christ addressing the seven churches in the opening chapters of Revelation. In v.3, Wesley carries the image beyond Paul's individual soldier to an appeal that the Christian army unite under 'Christ your head' (v.3.8), but he uses Paul's own appeal, "Let this mind be in you, which was also in Christ" (*Philippians 2:5*).

The verses about the armour and weapons were omitted from the 1780 hymnbook, and only the all-important shield of faith is mentioned (v.4.1, 2). In v.4.3 Wesley quotes from Milton's "Paradise Lost":

> Satan, with vast and haughty strides advanced,
> Came towering, armed in adamant and gold.

But Wesley gives the words a clever twist, for he is describing the Christian's impenetrable and valuable armour *against* Satan! Faith is in the crucified Christ (v.5.1) whose blood is "able to quench all the fiery darts of the wicked" (v.4.8)—an elaboration of *Ephesians 6:16*. We are to believe the Christ who said "neither shall any man pluck them out of my hand" (v.5.4; *John 10:28*) and "all power is given unto me" (v.5.6; *Matthew 28:18*). Wesley exhorts us 'Believe yourselves to heaven'.

In verse 6 Wesley introduces the theme of prayer in the words of Jesus in Gethsemane, "watch and pray" (*Mark 13:33, 37*). We are to 'pray without ceasing' (v.7.1-8; *1 Thessalonians 5:18*). We are to 'call upon the Lord' (v.7.4; *Isaiah 55:6*); and v.7.7 reminds us that "men ought always to pray and not to faint" (*Luke 18:1*).

"Let us come boldly to the throne of grace" (*Hebrews 4:16*). Verse 8 is certainly bold. We are to 'besiege his throne' (v.8.3). With the Psalmist we "pray for the peace of Jerusalem" (v.9.4; *Psalm 122:6*). Wesley refers to the incident when Moses' arms were supported as he prayed to God (*Exodus 9:29-33*) and expands the picture (v.9.7, 8).

'Wrestle . . . fight . . . pray . . . win' (v.10.1-4)—we return to *Ephesians 6* in the last verse. But we also glimpse the end of the battle and the conquest: "And the Spirit and the bride say, Come" (v.10.5, 6; *Revelation 22:17*); "I will come again, and receive you unto myself, that where I am, there ye may be also" (v.10.7, 8; *John 14:3*).

THOU HIDDEN SOURCE OF CALM REPOSE

"Christ is all and in all" (*Colossians 3:11*)

1 Thou hidden source of calm repose,
Thou all-sufficient Love Divine,
My help and refuge from my foes,
Secure I am, if thou art mine;
And lo! from sin, and grief, and shame,
I hide me, Jesus, in thy name.

2 Thy mighty name salvation is,
And keeps my happy soul above;
Comfort it brings, and power, and
peace,
And joy, and everlasting love;
To me, with thy dear name, are given
Pardon, and holiness, and heaven.

3 Jesu, my all in all thou art;
My rest in toil, my ease in pain,
The medicine of my broken heart,
In war my peace, in loss my gain,
My smile beneath the tyrant's frown,
In shame my glory and my crown:

4 In want, my plentiful supply,
In weakness my almighty power,
In bonds my perfect liberty,
My light in Satan's darkest hour,
In grief my joy unspeakable,
My life in death, my heaven in hell.

This hymn was first published in "Hymns and Sacred Poems", 1749, with the heading "Trust and Confidence". In the 1780 hymnbook it is in the section "For believers rejoicing". The theme of the hymn is so all-embracing that it could equally have a place in many other sections, for example, "For believers praying" and "For believers suffering".

The theme of this hymn is the all-sufficiency of Jesus. The title 'Love Divine' (v.1.2) is used in this hymn as in the better-known "Love Divine, all loves excelling" (p.52); this title encompasses all the attributes of Christ.

Jesus is help, refuge, and security to the Christian (v.1.3, 4). This is not a retreat from the real world: part of the source of v.1 is found in a Psalm that speaks later of treading on "the lion and the adder": "He that dwelleth in the secret place of the most High shall abide under the shadow of the almighty. I will say of the Lord: He is my refuge and my fortress: my God; in him will I trust" (*Psalm 91:1, 2*).

'Thy name' (v.1.6) is a favourite theme of Charles Wesley, found also in "Come, O thou traveller unknown" (p.32) and "Jesus, the name high over all" (p.46). Here, in v.1, 'thy name' is a hiding-place from sin, grief and shame (v.1.5, 6), but in v.2 'thy *mighty* name . . . brings . . . power' (v.2.1; 3). The name "Jesus" literally means "Saviour" (*Matthew 1:21*), hence the claim, 'thy name salvation is' (v.2.1), and the gifts of 'pardon and holiness and heaven' (v.2.6). Happiness, comfort, peace, joy and love are all in this verse: all are words inseparably linked with the name, character and promises of Jesus.

Verses 3 and 4 explore further the all-sufficiency of Jesus: 'Jesu, my all in all thou art' (v.3.1; *Colossians 3:11,* quoted opposite). Many human problems are listed: toil, pain, war, loss, tyranny, shame, want, weakness, bonds, darkness, grief, and death. All were familiar features in the eighteenth century: man has not solved any of them in two centuries of "progress", and some have even become more terrible. For each, Wesley finds a word from the Bible to offer Christian hope. He was probably also drawing on some words of St. Augustine (354-430), the North African bishop who was one of the most influential figures in the early church. His writings were familiar to the Wesleys, and in his "Soliliquies", St. Augustine wrote: "I am ill, I call for the doctor: I am blind, I hasten to the light: I am dead, I sigh for life. Thou art doctor, thou light, thou life, Jesus of Nazareth, have pity on me."

An alternative final couplet is found in some hymnbooks:

"My help and stay whene'er I call,
My life in death, my all in all"

thus returning to the assertion of v.3.1 and stressing again the theme of the whole hymn "Christ is all and in all" (*Colossians 3:11*).

YE SERVANTS OF GOD, YOUR MASTER PROCLAIM

"All thy works shall praise thee, O Lord; and thy saints shall bless thee. They shall speak of the glory of thy kingdom, and talk of thy power; to make known to the sons of men his mighty acts, and the glorious majesty of his kingdom."

(*Psalm 145:10-12*)

---

1 Ye servants of God, Your Master proclaim,
And publish abroad His wonderful name;
The name all-victorious Of Jesus extol;
His kingdom is glorious, And rules over all.

2 The waves of the sea Have lift up their voice,
Sore troubled that we In Jesus rejoice;
The floods they are roaring, But Jesus is here;
While we are adoring, He always is near.

3 Men, devils engage, The billows arise,
And horribly rage, And threaten the skies:
Their fury shall never Our steadfastness shock,
The weakest believer Is built on a Rock.

4 God ruleth on high, Almighty to save;
And still he is nigh, His presence we have;
The great congregation His triumph shall sing,
Ascribing salvation To Jesus our King.

5 "Salvation to God Who sits on the throne,"
Let all cry aloud, And honour the Son;
The praises of Jesus The angels proclaim,
Fall down on their faces, And worship the Lamb.

6 Then let us adore, And give him his right,
All glory and power, All wisdom and might,
All honour and blessing, With angels above,
And thanks never-ceasing, And infinite love.

This hymn was first published in "Hymns for times of trouble and persecution" in 1744. In that book, it had six verses and was in the section "Hymns to be sung in a tumult". It was not included in the 1780 hymnbook, but five verses appeared in a later supplement, in a section entitled "Worship". The verses about the "tumults" (vv.2, 3) are now normally omitted; it is sometimes claimed that they originally referred not to storms, but to the return of the 'Young Pretender' to Britain. Some hymnbooks set out the verses of this hymn in four lines (10.10.11.11), and some in eight short lines (5.5.5.5.6.5.6.5.).

God's "service is perfect freedom" says an ancient prayer. The relationship of master and servant (v.1.1) is a much happier one in a Christian context than in other circumstances. Thus the servants are happy to be called on to 'publish abroad his wonderful name' (v.1.2). In *Isaiah 9:6* we read, "his name shall be called wonderful". The 'all-victorious' name of Jesus (v.1.3) is a rephrasing of *Philippians 2:10*, ". . . at the name of Jesus every knee should bow", for 'he rules over all' (v.1.4). Christians are called to proclaim "the glorious majesty of his kingdom" (*Psalm 145:12*—see opposite).

The two verses about the storm, although normally omitted now, link well with the last words of v.1. They may also explain the choice of rhythm, which can convey the feeling of a storm. The verses blend the words of a Psalm with two passages in the Gospels: ". . . O Lord, the floods have lifted up their voice; the floods have lifted up their waves. The Lord on high is mightier than the noise of many waters, yea, than the mighty waves of the sea." (v.2,1, 3; 3.1-3; *Psalm 93:3-4*). In *Matthew 14:24-33* we can read about Jesus calming the storm, while in the Sermon on the Mount, the phrase 'built on a rock' (v.3.4), is another expression of confidence (*Matthew 7:24-5*).

The thoughts of v.4 can be found in the Psalms and in Revelation. The verse starts with a reaffirmation of God's power, as in *Psalm 93:4*. 'Mighty to save' (v.4.1) comes from *Isaiah 63:1*. The concept is also found in the Psalms: "He will fulfil the desire of them that fear him: he also will hear their cry and will save them" (*Psalm 145:19*). The previous verse of that Psalm asserts, "The Lord is nigh unto all them that call upon him"; Wesley adds the word 'still', and reinforces the phrase with the bold assertion 'His presence we have' (v.4.2). Thus we praise him: 'the great congregation' (v.4.3) can mean Christians on earth, "My praise shall be of thee in the great congregation" (*Psalm 22:25*), and also "a great multitude which no man can number of all nations and kindreds and people and tongues" (*Revelation 7:9-10*) in heaven.

Verse 5 starts with a quotation, indicated by the inverted commas, from the words of that "great multitude": "Salvation to our God, which sitteth upon the throne, and unto the Lamb" (*Revleation 7:10*). Lines 3 and 4 of this verse are also based on this passage: "the angels . . . fell before the throne on their faces, and worshipped God" (*Revelation 7:11*). In the final verse, Wesley develops this theme by inviting us to join in the praise: 'Let us adore' (v.6.1). The words come from the angels' song in *Revelation 7:12*: "Blessing and glory and wisdom and thanks-giving and honour and power and might be unto our God for ever and ever, Amen." Our thanks should truly be 'never ceasing' (v.6.4).

JESUS, THE FIRST AND LAST

"I am the Alpha and Omega, the first and the last"
(*Revelation 1:11*)

---

1 Jesus, the first and last,
On thee my soul is cast:
Thou didst thy work begin
By blotting out my sin;
Thou wilt the root remove,
And perfect me in love.

2 Yet when the work is done,
The work is but begun:
Partaker of thy grace,
I long to see thy face;
The first I prove below,
The last I die to know.

This hymn was first published in 1762 in "Short Hymns on Select Passages of Holy Scripture". The heading was "Present peace; anticipated joy". It was not included in the first edition of "Wesley's Hymns" (1780), but was added in later supplements.

Despite its brevity, the hymn is a masterpiece of poetry. There are only 63 words, and the vocabulary is extremely simple, but the meaning of the hymn is profound and Wesley weaves in phrases from different parts of the Bible. The whole hymn is a balanced development of the first line, 'Jesus, the first and last'. Both verses explore in lines 2-5 the meaning of 'Jesus, the first', and in lines 1 and 6 the meaning of 'Jesus, the last'.

The starting-point is *Revelation 1:11*, the words of the "one like unto the Son of Man" (*Revelation 1:13*). In the first verse, there is a dramatic contrast between the great vision of Christ as Eternal God in line 1 and Christ as individual saviour in line 2, yet this contrast is at the heart of the Gospel. *Psalm 40:22* promises, "Cast thy burden upon the Lord, and he shall sustain thee". In lines 3 and 4, Jesus the Saviour has answered the prayer of the penitent to "Hide my transgressions, and blot out all mine iniquities" (*Psalm 51:9*). Sin must be "rooted out", not just "pruned" (compare with *Matthew 3:10* and 15:13). The Christian is to be "rooted . . . in love" (*Ephesians 3:17*). The verse concludes with the reminder that perfect love is Christ's aim for us (see *1 John 4:12*).

Verse 2 reflects further on this apparent paradox of the Christian faith. 'The work' (v.2.1) of blotting out sin (i.e. justification) is indeed complete in the Christian. Yet 'the work' of removing sin (i.e. sanctification) is 'but begun' (v.2.2). Paul wrote "He which hath begun a good work in you will perform it until the day of Jesus Christ" (*Philippians 1:6*) and "Ye all are partakers of my grace" or ". . . partakers with me of grace" (*Philippians 1:7* and A.V. margin—v.2.3). This is a present-day truth: 'I prove (it) below' (v.2.5). V.2.4 reminds us of Paul's "desire to depart and be with Christ" (*Philippians 1:23*). The promise of *Revelation 12:4*, "They shall see his face" can be claimed only after death (v.2.6). "Now we see as in a glass darkly; but then, face to face" (*1 Corinthians 13:12*), so "For me to live is Christ, and to die is gain" (*Philippians 1:21*).